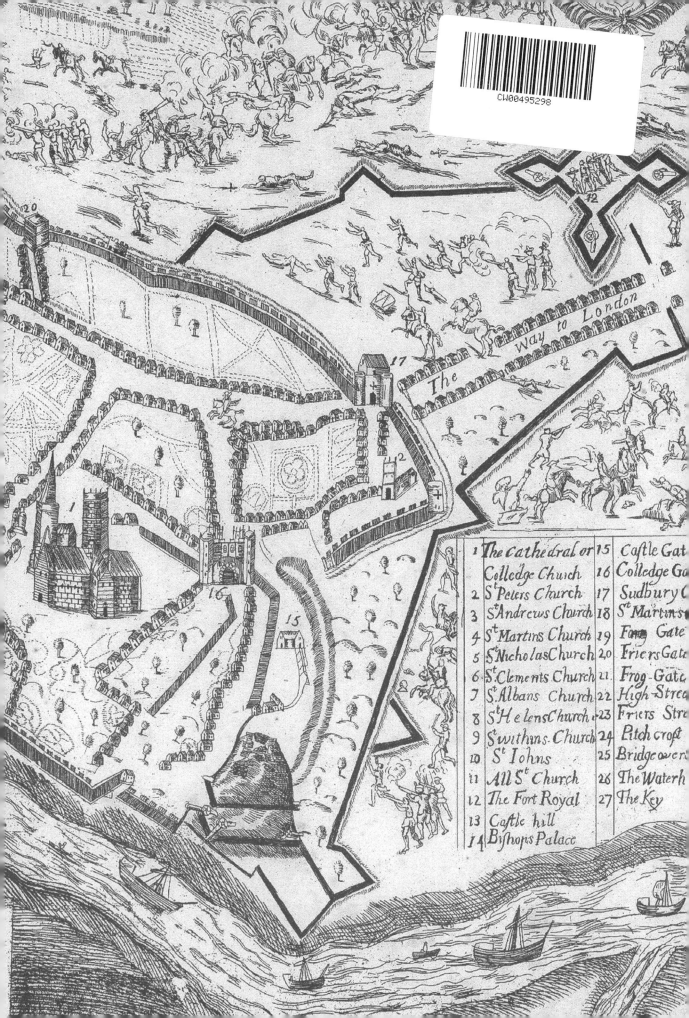

The Way to London

1	The Cathedral or Colledge Church	15	Castle Gat
2	St Peters Church	16	Colledge Ga
3	St Andrews Church	17	Sudbury (
4	St Martins Church	18	St Martins
5	St Nicholas Church	19	Fann Gate
6	St Clements Church	20	Friers Gate
7	St Albans Church	21	Frog-Gate
8	St Helens Church	22	High Stree
9	St withins Church	23	Friers Stre
10	St Iohns	24	Pitch croft
11	All St Church	25	Bridge over
12	The Fort Royal	26	The Waterh
13	Castle hill	27	The Key
14	Bishops Palace		

WORCESTER WITHIN THE WALLS

Clive R Haynes

The 'Changing Face of Worcester' Series

Series Editor Michael Fardon

OSBORNE HERITAGE

INSIDE FRONT COVER
Map of Worcester as it stood fortified on 3 September 1651, the eve of the Battle of Worcester.

INSIDE BACK COVER
Detail from map of Worcester, 1928.

Published by Osborne Books Limited
Unit 1B Everoak Estate, Bromyard Road
Worcester WR2 5HN

Printed by the Bath Press, Bath

British Library Cataloguing in Publication Data
A catalogue record for this book is available from the British Library

ISBN 1 872962 21 1

CONTENTS

Acknowledgements and Picture Credits   2

Foreword   3

Introduction   5

1   The Pattern of the Past – Blackfriars to Deansway   10

2   The Great Water Highway   56

3   Cathedral and Castle   90

4   The Pattern of the Past – The Foregate to Sidbury   104

Sources and References   154

Index   155

ACKNOWLEDGEMENTS AND PICTURE CREDITS

In producing this book I have received help and encouragement from many people. I would like to thank in particular my wife, Gill, for her support and her help in research, checking, proof reading and in keeping me on track. Thanks must also go to the County Archivist, Tony Wherry and his staff who have been so constantly helpful and supremely professional; to Pat Hughes, a glowing bundle of energy, whose extensive knowledge about structural aspects of the City has been invaluable; to The Dean and Chapter of Worcester Cathedral; to Trevor Lloyd-Adams, Manager of Crowngate and his staff, and to the many people who have permitted me to copy old pictures and documents and who have given me access during my researches to property and buildings. I am also indebted to Viking Publicity Limited for permission to reproduce the map shown on page 9. Lastly I would like to thank Jon Moore of Osborne Books for his help and advice in setting out the pages and Michael Fardon for holding the editorial helm.

Where the photographer is known, his or her initials appear first, followed by letters indicating the source. Where the identity of the photographer is not known. only the source is shown. Sometimes the photographer and the source are one and the same.

ADMcG	A.D. McGuirk	JJC	John J. Cam
AJB	A.J. Ballard	JMcC	J. McCowan
ALL	A. L. Lill.	JPF	J. Parkes Foy
BC	Bernard Croad	KB	Ken Beard
BG	Blackfriars (research) Group	MH	Malcolm Haynes
BWJ	Berrows Worcester Journal	MS	Mrs. Simpkins.
CK	Cyril Kershaw	N	Mr. Neat
CMHC	Clive and Malcolm Haynes Collection	RJC	R. J. "Jack" Collins
CRH	Clive R. Haynes	RN-J/MH	Richard Neilsen-Jones/Mr. & Mrs.Houghton
CRH/MH	Clive and Malcolm Haynes	TWM	T.W. Marsden
DF	Dennis Firkins	T	Mr. Tipton
DP	David Postle	WCL	Worcester City Library
ECH	Eric C. Hodson	WC	Worcester Cathedral
GNH	Geoffrey N. Hopcraft	WCM	Worcester City Museum
HS	Harry Sargeant	WEN	Worcester Evening News
HWCRO	Hereford and Worcester County Record Office	WWH	Walter W. Harris
JC	John Cam		

FOREWORD

There can be few people in Worcester or in the surrounding county who have not heard of, or who have not seen and experienced, the superb audio-visual presentation "The Changing Face of Worcester" by Clive and Malcolm Haynes. It is a real delight to be able to welcome this follow-on book version, written and compiled by Clive.

Much of the material in this volume is new, and relates to the approximate area of the City as it stood within its medieval walls. Today we think of our urban built-up areas as being somewhat unchanging and static, but in this volume we see how rapidly buildings, streets and places really do alter, in – historically speaking – a very short space of time.

Change is ever-present and inevitable in our society. Sadly so much goes unrecorded, despite the efforts of archivists, archaeologists and museum staff. As the person responsible for the maintenance of the County's written heritage -- whether in traditional documentary, photographic, or machine-readable form – nothing gives me greater pleasure than to see the publication of this volume.

A M Wherry, BA, DAA, County Archivist

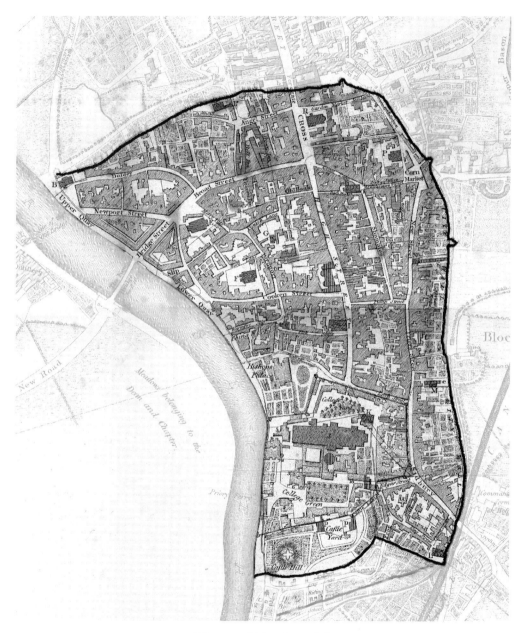

"Worcester Within the Walls"
An indication of the extent of Worcester City walls, from a map by Valentine Green, 1795.

INTRODUCTION

I first became fascinated by Worcester's past in 1964 when my brother Malcolm and I climbed the Cathedral tower to obtain a better view of the City, particularly the re-development of the Lich Street area. It was fortunate that about the same time we had become interested in photography. Looking out across the rooftops and seeing the intricate pattern of the streets, we decided to photograph the progress of the development. This intention was almost immediately linked to the questions about the past: why had the City evolved in the way it had? Could we find out more about our heritage? Could we, by using photography, better understand the growth of the City? We had no idea, but we resolved to find out. We contacted the City Librarian and Museum Curator, Cyril Phipps. He gave us great encouragement and fired our enthusiasm both for documenting the City on film and for copying material relevant to our researches. Very soon we realised that we had an enormous task on our hands. It surprised us that no-one before had undertaken such an in-depth, photographically comparitive approach to the study of Worcester. We realised that, in effect, we had begun a lifetime's work.

In 1967 we staged the first of our "Changing Face of Worcester" audio-visual shows. The shows became gradually more sophisticated over the years and now after almost thirty years, modern computer technology enables the use of seven projectors with a sixteen feet wide screen. Over the years some fifty thousand people have seen the show.

Our first book, co-authored with Brian Adlam, appeared in 1976 and our second, "Old Worcester as seen through the Camera", in 1985, was by Malcolm and myself. 1985 saw the production of another "parallel" major audio-visual show, "Worcester Cathedral in Focus", which was the culmination of two years research and photography. In this production we were assisted by my wife Gill and our photographer colleague, Martin Addison. In 1995 I co-produced a video with John Guy FRCS, entitled "Worcester the Faithful City".

This book is planned to be part of "The Changing Face of Worcester" series and has enabled me to take a more detailed look at specific areas and topics within the City. So, at last, it is possible to explore the development and changes that have taken place within certain defined limits without having to skip about the City giving a fragment from one area then another. Having made this statement, however, space can only permit so much and this volume might be seen as a pint pot into which a quart of history has been squeezed.

The "limits" referred to are the medieval City walls shown in the map on the opposite page. For readers who are not familiar with this boundary, we now take an imaginary tour around the walls. This tour starts at Sidbury and continues in a clockwise direction. The Sidbury Gate was the entrance to the City from the road to London and stood near to the present canal bridge. From here the wall proceeded westward to enclose St. Peter's Church and then joined the castle rampart (the King's School area) and continued on to the riverside. Along the river bank there was no defined line of walls, the river itself forming a natural defence. There were however some walls to protect exposed sections. The walls commenced again at the old bridge which was defended by a central tower. We must remember that the bridge at that time was further upstream than the present bridge and spanned the river from Tybridge Street to Newport Street. From the river bridge the wall ran eastwards along The Butts and Shaw Street to The Foregate. The Foregate was the main entrance to the City from the north. The wall then followed the south side of Sansome Street (once called Town Ditch) to cross Lowesmoor and proceed along Watercourse Alley (in effect, the northern end of City Walls Road). Across from Silver Street was the eastern entrance – St. Martin's Gate – and close by, a postern-gate, known as Clapgate. The walls then continued south, bordering properties to the east of New Street and Friar Street and so back to Sidbury. The Commandery stood just outside the Sidbury Gate and at one time provided rest for travellers arriving after the hour of closing. This last length of wall had no defensive tower, but there was a military blockhouse, added during the Civil War and this structure gave its name to the nearby district. This concludes our tour of the walls.

To help clarify the changing shape of the City, maps dated 1741, 1822 and 1991 are reproduced on the next three pages.

I sincerely hope that you enjoy this book and that it will help in furthering a deeper appreciation of our heritage. Worcester is a fine City and certainly one to be proud of. We must therefore strive to ensure that the glow of its past continues to illuminate its future.

Clive R. Hedges.

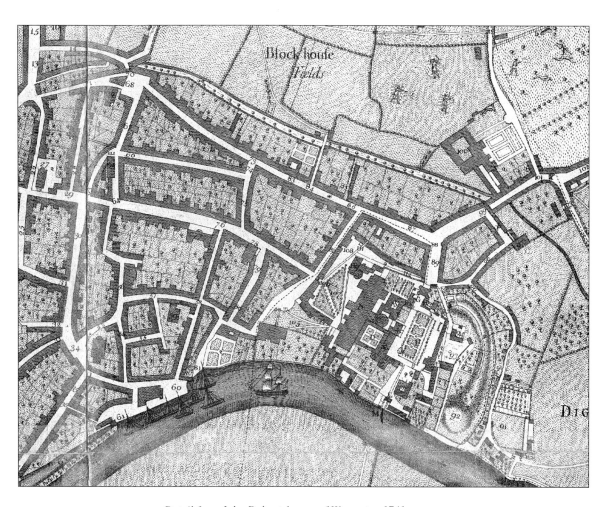

Detail from John Doharty's map of Worcester, 1741. (HWCRO).

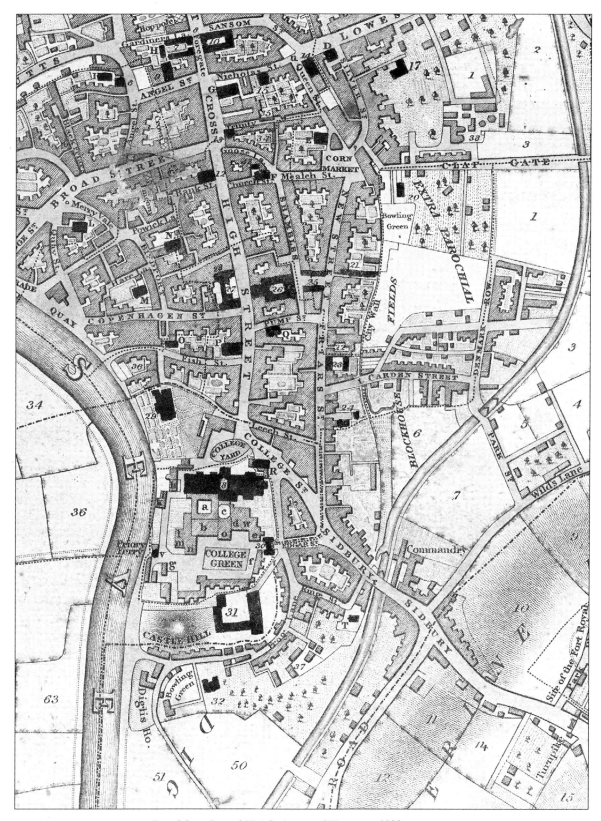

Detail from Samuel Mainley's map of Worcester, 1822. (HWCRO).

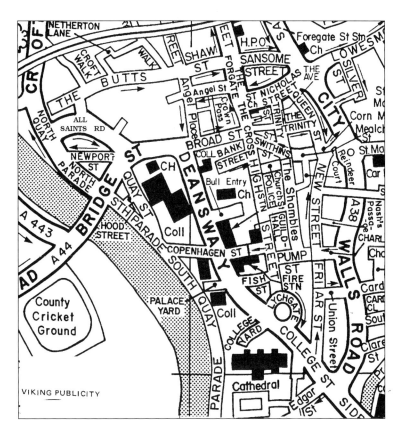

Worcester, 1991. Map reproduced by kind permission of Viking Publicity Limited.

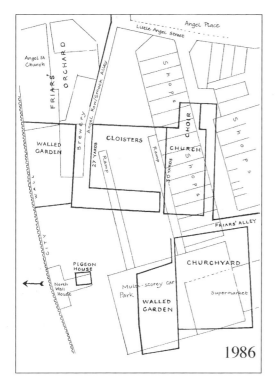

ABOVE
Aerial view, 1931 showing the extensive Cattle Market (centre), Dolday and the Watermans' Church with the curve of Dolday emerging at Broad Street (above All Saints Church, bottom right). Pemberton's brush factory rises amidst the clutter of Blackfriars. Newport Street shows a cleared area and South Parade construction work and new bridge building underway. To the right, above the railway viaduct, stands Worcester Royal Infirmary. (CMHC).

LEFT
Plan of Blackfriars area (1986) with the Dominican Friary outlines superimposed. (BG).

1

THE PATTERN OF THE PAST – BLACKFRIARS TO DEANSWAY

This opening chapter covers part of the area enclosed by the ancient City Wall and takes as its outer limits The Butts to the north, Angel Place and High Street to the east, All Saints Road to the west and Deansway and the Cathedral to the south. The district embraces a wealth of the City's heritage and the pictorial evidence may well be described as revealing a "Pattern of the Past". This area has been the site of extensive development and re-development during the last thirty years. In the process, archaeological evidence has given us valuable insights into the past, but regrettably by far the largest proportion of the original streets and buildings has been destroyed by successive developers and bulldozers.

Many older citizens can still recall the hurly-burly of daily life within a close-knit community. The now-vanished courts and alleyways spread like a web that linked the various districts, from the narrow Bull Entry and Chapel Walk, through the confines of Birdport and Merryvale, into All Hallows, The Well and so to Dolday. The complex warren of Blackfriars encompassed Friars' Alley, Morton Square, Rack Alley and Smock Alley to Little Angel Street.

For centuries this part of the City grew in a seemingly haphazard way, unrestricted by planning requirements and until the mid-part of the twentieth century, its almost organic and even symbiotic evolution could be traced from the pattern and layout of the inter-connecting passageways and streets. Much of this area was levelled during the 1930s in slum clearance schemes. At about the same time, Deansway was pushed through from Palace Yard via Birdport and Merryvale, so widening the route from the Cathedral to Bridge Street. Thirty years later, All Saints Road swept across Newport Street and Dolday. The Blackfriars warren was cleared and in its place arose the austere concrete and steel of Blackfriars Shopping Precinct. Now this in its turn has been superseded by the more elegant "Crowngate", which extends across the area to Bull Entry.

The sprawl of these modern developments is there for all to see, but how did this area develop and prosper in the way it did? Original settlements, which can be traced back for some two thousand years, grew up around the ford across the tidal Severn, probably just to the south of the Cathedral. The settlement flourished and commerce was stimulated when a bridge was built nearby, spanning the river from the bottom of Tybridge Street to Newport Street (once known as Eyeport). A defensive ditch and bank was erected to fortify the growing city and eventually stone walls were built. In 1347, on a stretch of land on the low ridge overlooking the Severn, Dominican friars established a friary in the area between what is now Dolday and Angel Place. They were known as "Blackfriars" because of their black habit. The Blackfriars Research Group suggested in 1986 that the friary church probably had a nave 116 ft long by 59 ft wide, with a quire 36 ft long by 29 ft wide. In addition there would have been a steeple and cloisters. Most was destroyed during the Dissolution in 1539. I am indebted to the Blackfriars Group for this information; a copy of their plan appears on the opposite page.

The Dominican Friary was only one of the developments within the area. As a rural cathedral City, administration centre, market and focal point for commerce, Worcester was a natural base for numerous trades. The City became pre-eminent in the country for the clothing trade, particularly during the 15th and 16th centuries when its broadcloth made it famous. In 1540, John Leland reported to King Henry VIII, "the welthe of the towne of Worcestor standithe most by draping and noe towne in England, at this present tyme, maketh so many cloathes yearly as this towne doth" (Extract from Leland's *Itinerary*).

The clothing industry centred on the Blackfriars area would have involved many skilled tradespeople. Here could be found weavers, drapers, hosiers, walkers, dyers, and many associated trades. A Clothiers Trade Guild was formed to regulate standards of practice and to act as a "mutual society". The various guilds participated in colourful pageants to display their authority as they processed through the City. The cloth trade gave its name to Smock Alley and Rack Alley. Racks were used in the manufacturing process, as wet cloth was hung to dry on long timber frames, generally known as tenter frames, though locally as "racks". The cloth was tensioned and stretched on rows of "tenter hooks" (from which the phrase, when under tension, "to be on tenter hooks" derives). The cloth trade in Worcester declined in the 17th century and finally ceased after the introduction of coal and steam powered mills in northern towns during the Industrial Revolution.

The district gradually became "industrialised" and more space was needed for housing. In time the enclosed squares and courts became considerably overcrowded, leading to slum conditions. Among the many businesses that flourished in the Blackfriars area were those of Pemberton's, Morton, Lewis Clarke's and James Ward. The brush manufacturing company of Abraham Pemberton & Son, was situated west of Friars Alley and was built over part of the old churchyard. Pemberton's made a wide range of brushes which included those for hair, teeth, scrubbing, the hearth, paint, blacking, clothes, brooms and for sweeps. A wide range of matting was manufactured too. The business flourished for a hundred and fifty years from the 1770s to the 1920s.

Richard Morton owned a timber yard in this area. Morton was a highly respected, influential and prominent citizen. He was a cabinet maker, undertaker and official carpenter to the Cathedral. He held high offices within the City and became Mayor in 1796. A local landmark for many years was the tall, square chimney of Lewis Clarke's Brewery. The company was established in 1902, when an agreement was made between Robert Clarke, William Price Hughes and Bertha Lewis, taking over the Upper Butts Brewery of James Allies. The buildings stood along the northern side of Smock Alley and fronted Angel Row/Angel Place. Latterly, Messrs. Marston's took over the business. Many residents can still recall James Ward's premises that fronted onto Broad Street. Wards were general ironmongers, heating engineers and radio and TV dealers.

To the south of Broad Street, the recent Crowngate development covers another historic though, perhaps, less cohesive part of the City. At the heart of this area was The Countess of Huntingdon's Church, which was established in 1773. The building we see today is, in fact, the second church on the site, the original having stood in the garden of a large town house. The area became increasingly populated by the poor and as such became a target for the evangelical drive of Selina, Countess of Huntingdon. To accommodate the increasing congregation a new church replaced the original in 1804. This was enlarged in 1815, the box pews being added in 1839. The building could hold 1,500 worshipers. In the immediate vicinity was a warren of streets and tenements teeming down to the riverside. For most of its history the Huntingdon Church was hidden away between Deansway, Chapel Walk, Powick Lane and Bull Entry. Following successive clearances the congregation diminished and the church finally closed its doors in 1976. After being redundant for many years, it now stands renovated in its new role as a concert hall, with the associated Elgar School of Music next door.

Like Blackfriars, the Deansway area contained a mixture of trades and industries. Between Copenhagen Street and Powick Lane, on the site presently occupied by the City Police Station,

Webb's Horsehair Carpet factory once stood. This four storey building at 8 Copenhagen Street, was built in the mid 18th century and was used for weaving and dying. The twenty seven year-old Edward Webb took over the premises in 1835 and within 10 years the business had expanded to boast twenty nine Jacquard looms. Large numbers of women and children were employed for the tasks of weaving; indeed their traditional outfits of shawls and cloggs gave the district quite a Lancashire mill town appearance. Edward, who became Mayor in 1847, was concerned for the education of children and in 1846, established the City's only factory school, an evening school initially for around 40 girls. Webb's Carpets were a famous Worcester "export"; Prime Minister Gladstone ordered carpets for Number 10 and six hundred yards of "grey Worcester" was ordered for the wedding of the Duke of York in 1893. In addition, Webb's horse-hair carpet foot rugs were used by most early railway companies in Britain. The factory moved to Sherriff Street premises in 1935.

Before the coming of Deansway in the 1930's, the district was connected by narrow roads that ran from All Saint's Church, (the area called The Well or All Hallow's), along Merryvale to Birdport and so southwards, crossing Copenhagen Street, to Little Fish Street, finally skirting The Old Palace via Palace Yard to emerge at the south end of High Street, opposite Lich Street. Birdport probably derived from "British Gate/British Port" and Merryvale/Merrievale from St. Mary's Vale, referring to the Cathedral which is dedicated to St. Mary.

Detail of Blackfriars area model showing the Dominican friary and graveyard (upper centre-middle), the diagonal run of the City Wall along The Butts and the racks for drying cloth. (CRH/BG).

Lewis Clarke's Brewery, Angel Place, 1895 with Smock Alley to the left hand side. (ADMcG/WCM).

Lewis Clarke's advert, 1895. (CMHC).

Lewis Clarke's Brewery. The coopers shop, c1900. (CMHC).

Brewery interior, c1900. (CMHC).

Angel Place, c1950, view to the north west, with Abell & Smith's, electrical co., Electra House, The Vaults Inn (licencees in 1955-56, Mr & Mrs C. A. Sier) and Lewis Clarke's Brewery. In the distance is The Five Ways Hotel with the Norwich Union offices to the right. (WCL).

Lewis Clarke's Brewery, Blackfriars, c1900, view to the east from North Wall House. Smock Alley runs between the wall and the cottages. The cottages to the right of centre, fronted onto Morton Square which was adjacent to Smock Alley. (CMHC)

From the same viewpoint, 7th March 1996. (CRH).

TOP
Angel Place c1855, view across The Sheepmarket area to the junction of Little Angel Street (left) and Angel Row (with Five Ways off to the right). At one time the whole length of both Little Angel Street and Angel Street was called Angel Lane. The Friars' orchard (c1500-1600) once covered land later occupied by Lewis Clarke's and the Congregational Church. At the extreme right is the Phoenix Fire Engine House, later The Norwich Union. To the right of the archway (which led via an alley, to the 1859 Congregational Church) is the Worcester Homoeopathic Dispensary, once the minister's house. To the left, the vestry and above the arch, Worcester's first subscription library. To the left of the picture is Lewis Clarke's Brewery. (WCM).

MIDDLE
Demolition of Lewis Clarke's buildings, 6th December 1970. (CRH).

BOTTOM
Angel Place and the Lewis Clarke's corner area, 29th March 1996. (CRH).

The Butts, view from the west, 15th March, 1958, from near the Ewe & Lamb Inn with the Cattle Market, on the left. (HS).

Pemberton's Brush Factory, Blackfriars, in the course of demolition, September, 1967 (RJC).

North Wall House along the southern side of The Butts, towers astride the old City Wall. This gaunt and characterful building stands near to the site of the "Cold Bath". The "Cold Bath" stream issued from here to flow across Pitchcroft and so into the Severn near where the railway bridge now stands. (See map). With waters publicised as "pure" such baths were for public bathing and washing, and became popular meeting places in the 18th century. In 1719, Shadrath Pride, an innkeeper acquired the lease and took advantage of the Georgian fashion for such centres. Shadrath also built a refreshment room for patrons, the "Banqueting Hall" as he called it, above the Cold Baths. Later, the building was enlarged and became a residence. In Victorian times it was Worcester's first Grammar School for Girls. (CRH).

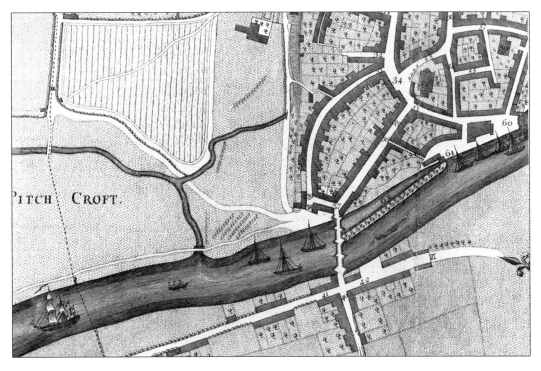

Detail from F. Doharty's map, 1741, showing the "Cold Bath Stream" along the east side of The Butts, crossing Pitchcroft, joining another flow and entering the Severn. (HWCRO).

Blackfriars multi-story carpark c1987, view from the east. North Wall House is to the right. (CRH).

Crowngate multi-storey carpark and 'bus station entrance, same viewpoint as in the above picture, 17th August, 1996. To the right, vestiges of Lewis Clarke's Brewery remain. Appropriately part of the one time brewery complex is now Barrels Wine Bar. (CRH).

ABOVE
Aerial view of City central area from the south-west, 1921.
Bottom left is Blackfriars with, to its right, Little Angel Street
cleared to the east side to become the much wider, Angel
Place. Under construction is Worcester Fruit and Vegetable
Market, previously The Sheep Market, at the corner of Five
Ways and Angel Street. (CMHC).

RIGHT
The north end of Little Angel Street c1912. The Vaults Hotel
is to the right. The sign states that all ales are brewed on the
premises! Thomas Prosser was the licencee. (CMHC).

RIGHT
The Bell Hotel at the south east corner of Little Angel Street and Broad Street, c1910. The narrow Little Angel Street had the line of properties on the east (The Cross side) demolished in 1913 , and from around 1920 the widened area formed Angel Place. The Bell was one of the many coaching inns in the City . (CMHC).

BELOW
Angel Place, view to the north from Broad Street, May 1978. (CRH).

BOTTOM
From the same viewpoint, 29th March 1996. (CRH).

The south west corner of Angel Place and Broad St. c1930. Charles Edwards, Wine Merchants fill the picture with the City Fruit Stores at the extreme right. The photographer was Richard Neilsen-Jones who owned the Horace Dudley Studio at 46, Broad Street. (RN-J/MH).

From the same viewpoint, 29th March 1996. (CRH).

ABOVE
Blackfriars area under development in 1968, view to NW from upper floor of A.O. Jones, corner of Angel Place and Broad Street. The tall building was once Pemberton's brush factory. (MH)

RIGHT
Men at work, Blackfriars, 30th May 1968. (CRH/MH).

BELOW
Blackfriars development, view to west from roof of the Scala cinema, 30th May 1968. In the distance, one of the high rise flats (Severn House) near Tybridge Street is under construction, clad in scaffolding (CRH/MH).

Aerial view in May 1978 centring on Dolday and Blackfriars. Newport Street Bus Station stands to the left. To the north side of The Butts is the City Streets Department depot with Netherton Lane curving around to run parallel with the railway viaduct. The arches of the viaduct are "home" to many small businesses, many connected with the motor repair trade. (CRH).

View to the north west from All Saint's Church tower, 1965. Newport Street leads down to the riverside and the Power Station still stands. All Saints Road was constructed in about 1967. (GNH).

North end of Angel Place in the late 1970's. Worcester Fruit & Vegetable Market (old Sheep Market) awaits re-development to become Angel Mall. The public conveniences to the right of the picture date back to the widening of the area - being constructed about 1913 (CRH).

The Scala Cinema opened in 1922. The foyer in 1973 (CRH/MH).

Scala cinema interior, May 1973 (CRH/MH).

Scala cinema, in the projection room with Manager, Mr. Rider and Projectionist, Mr. Griffiths, 31st May 1973. The Cinema closed a few days later. (CRH/MH).

Scala cinema interior, May 1973 (CRH/MH).

Blackfriars construction, view to the north from the tower of All Saints Church, Broad Street, 1967. (CRH/MH).

Similar view, 7th March 1996, with Crowngate occupying the Blackfriars area. (CRH).

Angel Place entrance to Blackfriars Shopping Centre c1987. Properties were closing down in readiness for re-development.
(CRH).

From the same viewpoint, March 1996. (CRH).

Blackfriars Shopping Centre c1987 with the Market Hall to the left and Safeway Supermarket at the far (western) end. (CRH).

From the same viewpoint in March 1996. (CRH).

The rather austere Blackfriars Shopping Centre in the 1980s, view to the south with Peter Richards' clothing shop to the left, a cycle shop to the right, at a time when National Express coach services were offering a return fare to London at £9. (CRH).

From the same viewpoint in March 1996. Friary Walk, Crowngate, presents a pleasant enclosed area for shoppers to browse. St. Andrew's Spire is visible through the glazed apex at the far end. (CRH).

Angel Place, view to the south west, c1987. Bus stops line the centre of Angel Place. (CRH).

From the same viewpoint, 17th August 1996. Market traders' brightly-coloured stalls occupy the site of the bus shelters.
(CRH).

Angel Street, view to the west, 1978. The gap to the left of Shakespeare Hotel, presently Kwik Save Supermarket, is where the Theatre Royal once stood. The angular Blackfriars car park rears in the near distance. (CMH).

Angel Street, from the same viewpoint, 29th March 1996, revealing more of the frontage of the Shakespeare Hotel. (CRH).

The Theatre Royal and Opera House c1930. The theatre was one of a succession on this site. This structure dates from 1877 following the fire that destroyed the 1875 building. The theatre's heyday was during the late 1700's and mid 1800's when Sarah Siddons, Edmund Keen, Young Roscium and the Kembles performed here. Grimaldi appeared too, as did Vesta Tilley, the Worcester born music-hall artiste. The theatre closed on 28th May 1955 and was demolished in 1962. Kwik Save supermarket is now on the site. (CMHC).

The interior of the Theatre Royal c1900. Stalls, Circle and "The Gods". (CMHC).

ABOVE LEFT.   Old Theatre Royal poster (CMHC).

ABOVE RIGHT   Vesta Tilley in military attire, c1890. Born Matilda Alice Powles in the Blockhouse area (near the canal along Park Street) of Worcester on 13th May 1864, she became a child performer at Worcester music halls with her father, an established entertainer.   A renowned male impersonator, she maintained contact with "her public", marrying into the nobility to become Lady de Frece. She died in 1952. (CMHC).

Angel Street and the Theatre Royal in the 1940's. (CMHC).

ABOVE
Broad Street, view to the east
from near entrance, on the
left, to Blackfriars, c1910.
An electric tram takes centre
stage whilst to the right
stands The Beauchamp
Hotel (Henry William Smith,
proprietor, 1912).
   (CMHC).

RIGHT
From the same viewpoint
in May 1978. (CRH/MH).

LEFT
From the same viewpoint,
17th August, 1996. (CRH).

Broad Street, 8th August, 1958, at the junction with Deansway. Both the premises of Modern Fireplaces (previously Thomas H. Hayes, furniture dealer) and G. A. Palmer & Son, fruiterer & florist (previously Laurence E. Sleath), were demolished. (CK).

Broad Street/Deansway corner 8th August 1958. An interesting picture as it shows the northern side of Broad St. We can discern No 28, W.H. Hopkins & Co., Bakers; No. 27 A.F. Eden, fruiterer & fishmonger and No. 26, Albion House, toy & woolshop. (CK).

Broad Street 29th March 1996. Elevated view to the east. (CRH).

ESTABLISHED   OF A
UPWARDS   CENTURY.

E. LEONARD'S
FAMILY GROCERY ESTABLISHMENT,
25, Broad Street, WORCESTER.

TEAS.

The present Duty on all descriptions of Tea is 1s. 6d. per pound; on April 5th,1855, it will be reduced to 1s. 3d. per pound; and on April 5th, 1856, to 1s. per pound.

Good ordinary Congou,	2	10
Good and strong ditto,	3	0
Strong rough-flavoured ditto	3	4
Superior ditto ditto,	3	8
Very fine Congou,	4	0
Pekoe-flavoured ditto,	4	4
Fine Pekoe ditto,	4	8
Souchong, from 3 8 to	4	8
Very fine Lapsang Souchong	5	0
Plain Orange Pekoe, from 3 4 to	4	4
Scented ditto ditto, very fine,	4	6
Twankay,	3	0
Hyson kind,	3	4
Hyson,	3	8
Good Hyson,	4	0
Fine Cowslip-flavoured ditto,	4	6
Very fine and rich Hyson, 5 0 to	6	0
Common Young Hyson,	3	0
Good ditto ditto	3	4
Superior ditto ditto,	4	0
Very fine ditto ditto	4	4
Rich and delicate ditto,	5	0
Imperial Gunpowder,	3	0
Good ditto, 3 4 to	3	8
Strong ditto,	4	0
Very strong ditto,	4	8
Fine Small Leaf ditto,	5	4
Finest Pearl Leaf ditto,	6	0

AGENT FOR

Howqua's Mixture,	5	0
Semi-Howqua,	4	4
Mowqua's Gunpowder,	6	8
Semi-Mowqua,	6	0

COFFEE.

This being an Article of such increasing consumption, has had a large share of my attention, both in its selection and the most approved process of Roasting, whereby the aromatic property, so essential in good Coffee, is preserved.

Ceylon Coffee, 10d. to	1	0
Plantation ditto,	1	2
Fine Berbice,	1	4
La Guayra,	1	4
Costa Rica,	1	4
Jamaica,	1	6
Fine Mountain ditto,	1	8
Ditto Mocha,	1	8
Old ditto,	1	10

LEONARD'S
Canister Coffees.

(In one and two lb. Canisters.)

Fine Plantation Coffee,	1	4
Ditto Jamaica,	1	8
Old Mocha,	1	10

Raw Coffee at all prices.
Smith's Essence of Coffee
In Bottles, at 1s. and 2s. each.

Cocoa and Chocolate.

These articles, so beneficial to Invalids, require great care in obtaining qualities pure from adulteration: this has been my principal study.

Leonard's Soluble Cocoa
Fry's ditto
White's ditto
Taylor's ditto
Feek's ditto
Plain ditto
Fry's Patent
White's Patent
Superior Cocoa Nibs
Ground Cocoa
Granulated Cocoa
Flake Cocoa
Loose Soluble
Homœopathic Cocoa
Sir Hans Sloane's Chocolate
Churchman's
White's
Leonard's Soluble
Fry's ditto
Taylor's ditto
French Chocolate
Chocolate Paste in ¼lb. pots
Ditto Powder in ½lb. canisters
Trinidad Chocolate

SUGARS.

Fine Jamaica or Raw Sugar
East India Sugar
Crystalized ditto
Mauritius ditto
Brown Lump ditto
Fine ditto ditto
Double refined ditto
Crushed Lump
Molasses
Golden Syrup
Brown Candy
White ditto

SPICES.

Mace
Ditto Ground
Cinnamon Bark
Ditto Ground
Cloves
Ditto Ground
Best mixed Spice

Fine Brown Nutmegs
White Nutmegs
Wild ditto
Cassia
Pimento
Black Pepper
White ditto
Cayenne ditto
Long ditto
Cake Spice
Caraways
Ground ditto
Corianders
Turmeric
Barbadoes Ginger
East India ditto
Jamaica ditto
Ground ditto
Cayenne Pods
Double superfine Mustard
Fine ditto
Seconds ditto
Leonard's Durham Mustard, (packed in tin foil) 1s. 6d. per lb., very superior.

PICKLES.

Piccalilli
Mixed Pickles
Onions
Gherkins
White Onions
Walnuts
Cauliflower
French Beans
Red Cabbage
Imperial Hot
Mushrooms
Superfine Capers

RICH SAUCES, &c.

Soho Sauce
Burgess' Essence of Anchovies
Browning Sauce
Essence of Lobster
Essence of Shrimps
Cocks' Reading Sauce
India Soy
China ditto in fancy vases
Lazenby's Harvey Sauce
Sir Robert Peel's Sauce
Warwickshire Sauce
Royal Table Sauce
Mushroom Ketchup
Ditto ditto, pints
Walnut ditto
Ditto, pints
Syrup of Lemon
Lemon Pickle
French Olives
Worcestershire Sauce
Tomata Sauce
Universal Sauce, pints

ABOVE AND NEXT PAGE
E. Leonard's extensive advertisement in Billing's Directory of 1855. (CMHC).

Ditto ditto, quarts
India Chetney
Soyer's Sauce
—— Zest
Curry Paste
Mulligatawny ditto
Essence of Almonds
Chilli Vinegar
Raspberry Vinegar
Stivens' Orange Tonic
French Truffles
Lemon Marmalade
Orange ditto
French Custard Powder
Salts of Lemon
French Gelatine
Preserved Ginger
Ditto dried ditto
Finest Salad Oil, in Flasks
India Curry Powder
Anchovies, real Gorgona
Anchovy Paste, &c., &c.

FOREIGN FRUITS.

Bunch Muscatels
Layer ditto
Ditto ditto, very fine
Valentia Raisins
Sultana ditto
Malaga ditto
Patras Currants
Zante ditto
Turkey Figs
Malaga ditto
Finest Eleme ditto
French Plums
Ditto ditto, fancy boxes
Prunes
Pistachio Kernels
Candied Orange Peel
Ditto Lemon ditto
Ditto Citron ditto
Crystal Fruit
Jordan Almonds
Valentia ditto
Bitter ditto
Fine Lemons

HOPS.

E. L. has at all times a Stock selected from the Choicest Growths, viz.:—
Fine New East Kents
Ditto Mid ditto
Ditto Farnhams
Ditto Sussex
Ditto Worcesters
Ditto Herefords
Ditto Mathon Whites
Ditto Cooper Whites
Prime Old Hops

Candles and Soaps.

Genuine Wax Candles
Ditto Sperm ditto
Ditto Margarine ditto
Wax Carriage Lights
Mixed Wax Tapers
Wax Bougies
Palmer's Metallic, 2 Wicks
Ditto ditto, 1 Wick
Ditto Magnum
Ditto Minimum
Ditto Batswing
Ditto Stripe Wick
Ditto Mid Size
Price's Patent Composite
Ditto Belmont ditto
Ditto ditto, Wax
Ditto ditto, Sperm
Decimal Palm Candles
Patent Cocoa Nut
Fairfield Sperm, Ditto Wax

Child's Night Mortars
Field's ditto
Albert Night Lights
Tins and Glasses for ditto
Kensington Moulds
Cotton Dips
Thread ditto
Rushlights
Brown Windsor Soap
White ditto
Rose Soap, Palm ditto
Castile ditto, Honey ditto
Egg Tablets, in Boxes
Best White Soap
—— Mottled ditto
Second ditto ditto
Best Yellow ditto
Second ditto
Third ditto ditto

MISCELLANIES.

East India Rice
Patna ditto
Carolina ditto
Ground ditto
Naples Maccaroni
Genoa Vermicelli
Tapioca, Pearl Sago
Finest Bermuda Arrow Root
Fine Jamaica ditto
Millet
Semolina
Huntley & Palmer's Biscuits
—— Reading
—— Arrow Root
—— Queen's
—— Machine
—— Pic-Nic
—— Caraway Tonbridge
—— Cracknells
—— Almond Drops
—— Ginger Wafer
—— Spice Nuts
—— Captains
—— Maccaroons
Hard's Farinaceous Food
Scotch and Pearl Barley
Finest Picked Isinglass
Brazil ditto
Nelson's Patent Gelatine
Robinson's Patent Groats
—————— Barley
Whole Groats, Embden Groats
Real Scotch Oatmeal
Derbyshire ditto
Alexander's Pea Flour
Baking Powder, Egg Powder
Split Peas
Lescher's Patent Starch
Ricketts' Soluble ditto
Glenfield Starch, Glaze ditto
Rice ditto, Poland ditto
London ditto
Best Stone Blue
Common ditto
Smalts
Washing Powder
—————— Soda
Saltpetre
—— Prunella
Bay Salt, Basket Salt
Scotch Snuff
Ditto Scented ditto
Welsh Snuff
Prince's Mixture
Black Rappee
Strasburg
Hardham's No. 37
Lundyfoot
Taddy's Brown Rappee
Best Bristol Rag Tobacco
Bird's Eye ditto

Roll ditto
Finest Alloa Roll
Bogie Roll
Broad Cut Tobacco
K'naster ditto
Yara ditto
Returns ditto
Franklyn's Bristol Rag
Amersfoot Cigars
Cubas, 9s. and 10s.
Havannah ditto, 12s., 14s., and 16s., very prime
Regalias
Estrellas
Foreign Cabanas
Ditto Woodvilles
Ditto Principees
Ditto Silvas
Ditto Havannahs
Ditto Manillas
Rape Seed, Canary ditto
Hemp ditto, Mustard ditto
Linseed
Millet Seed
Juice, Solazzi
—— Baracco
—— Refined
Chamomile Flowers
Senna, Epsom Salts
Cochineal
Prepared ditto
Carbonate of Soda
Tartaric Acid
Cudbear
Orris Root
Alkanet ditto
Malt Liquor Reviver
Worcester Malt Vinegar
London ditto ditto
Finest French ditto
White Wine ditto
Distilled ditto
Sulphur and Roll Brimstone
Fullers' Earth
Rotten Stone
Ground ditto in packets
Calais Sand
Whiting, Pipe Clay
Walker's Percussion Caps
Patent Shot
Ivory Black
Venetian Red
Mexican Black Lead
Leonard's Pencil ditto
Housemaids' Gloves
Glue and Bees' Wax
Liquid Blacking
Paste ditto
Chalk, Alum
Wafers
Stephens' Writing Fluid
Black Ink in small bottles
Red ditto ditto
Emery Cloth, Emery Powder
Emery and Sand Paper
White Plate Powder
Pale Rouge ditto
Furniture Polish, Brass Polish
Bath Bricks, Hearth Stones
Annatto or Cheese Colouring
White and Brown Paper
Prime Welsh Butter
—— Irish ditto

BRITISH WINES.

Ginger
Orange
Raisin
Cowslip } 15s. per doz.
Stivens' Green Ginger and all other British Wines

Families residing in the country will find an advantage in dealing at the above Establishment, as the Proprietor has entered into arrangements for supplying general Family Orders (for prompt payment) Carriage Free.
ORDERS PER POST OR CARRIER CAREFULLY AND PROMPTLY ATTENDED TO.

Broad Street, c1900. Narrow Little Angel Street can just be seen between the premises of Dingle, Son & Edwards, Wine Importers, and The Bell Hotel. (WWH/HWCRO).

Abell & Smith's Electrical Co. Ltd., advertisement, c1930. (CMHC).

The south east corner of Angel Place and Broad Street, c1930. Jap Co. on the corner were furniture dealers; next was the Post Office, then Halfords. In the distance is the conical roof of The International Stores at The Cross. To the right of the picture stand the offices of Berrow's Worcester Journal. (CMHC).

A deserted Broad Street scene in December 1939. A.O. Jones at the left of the picture were advertising an Xmas Bazaar. (JPF/GNH).

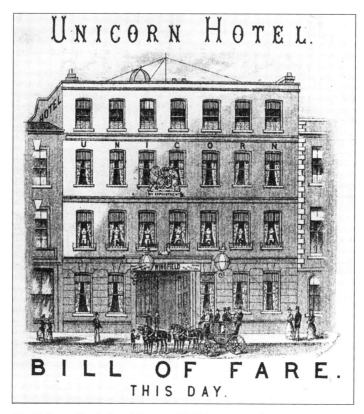

The Unicorn Hotel, Broad Street, mid-19th century. Once a coaching inn, the hotel eventually became Unicorn Chambers and housed a variety of shops and enterprises. (CMHC).

Broad Street, 17th August, 1996. The Crowngate portico now fronts onto what was the Unicorn Hotel. (CRH/MH)

Broad Street, view to the west from The Cross c1906. The ornate posts that carried the current for the electric tramway are evident as is The Crown Hotel to the right. Next to the Crown is Thomas Edwin Blackford's drapery establishment advertising jackets and mantles and "The Worcester Mourning Warehouse". Further down, a pair of eyes stare out from the first floor – the premises of James Lucking & Co. Opticians; next is the Bell Hotel (Thomas Stanley D'Aeth). To the left of the picture at number 62, Herbert E. Pollard & Co., practical gun makers, at 61, Miss H.H. Burrow, Corset Maker. (CMHC)

Broad Street, an elevated view to the west from The Cross c1952. On the left is the corner site occupied by the Midland Bank (ground floor) and Pearl Assurance (upper floor). Glenn's the gentlemen's outfitters is next down the street, then Richard Shirley Skan's & Sons, tobacconists and gentlemen's hairdressers. (CMHC).

ABOVE

Broad St., south side in 1958. Skan's shop (Post Office in 1912) can be seen and that of H.S. Coverdale, trading as George & Welch, pharmacists (No 68). In these premises Worcestershire Sauce was first produced for sale by Lea & Perrins in 1837. (GNH).

RIGHT

The corner of Broad Street and The Cross, c1850. (CMHC).

BELOW

A similar view, 3rd April 1996. The brick frontage, a little way down on the right hand side, of The Abbey National Bank, was previously occupied by Mothercare, before that the site was Beard's food emporium, a double fronted shop of considerable character. (CRH).

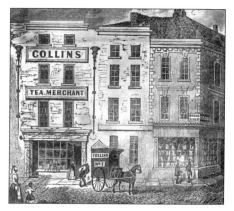

Broad Street, junction with Newport Street, c1960's. The James Cafe was just at the junction, with the Herefordshire House Inn the next door down Newport Street. (CMHC)

Junction of Broad Street and All Saints Road, 29th March, 1966. The "rump" of Newport Street can be seen beyond the traffic lights. Some of the properties shown in the picture at the top of the page were demolished to allow the construction of All Saints Road. The Take 'A' Break Cafe is the property seen to the extreme right of the upper picture. (CRH).

Newport Street, view from north west, c1905, (WCM) a water colour by local artist, Evacustes Phipson. Around that time, besides the Herefordshire House, other pubs included, the Old Red Lion (No 18), the Green Dragon (No 44) and the Hope and Anchor, now The Severn View Hotel (No 54). A listing from the Worcester Directory of 1912 (shown at the bottom of the page) gives something of the flavour of the street, its courts and tenants.

Newport Street, view from the north west, Courts 3 & 4, c1931. This picture was taken at the time of slum clearance in the area. (ADMcG/WCM).

NEWPORT STREET.

RIGHT SIDE FROM BROAD STREET
2 James & Son, fruiterers, &c.
4 Westwood Ben, *Herefordshire House Inn*
6 Barnett John, Ltd., corn & meal factors (see advt.)
8 Green William, shopkeeper
10 *Void*
12 Link Henry, shopkeeper
14 Thornborrow Geo. Ellison, clothes dlr.
HERE IS COURT No. 1
16 *Void*
18 Sefton George W., *Old Red Lion Inn*
HERE IS COURT No. 2
20 & 22 Strickland Henry, regd. lodging house
HERE IS COURT No. 3
24 Lucy Joseph, bricklayer
HERE IS COURT No. 4
26 Hughes George, carter
28 Humphries Charles, shopkeeper
30 Warr Ed., labourer

HERE IS COURT No. 5
36 Browne Mrs. Eliza
38, 38A & 40 Band Wm., marine store dealer and lodgings
42 Dax Henry, common lodging house
44 Bennett George, *Green Dragon Inn*
46 Perks John, yardsman
48 Let to various tenants
50 Lane Mrs. Sarah
52 Bull Mrs.
54 Harper Jesse, *Hope and Anchor*
HERE IS NORTH QUAY
11 Parnam Thomas
9 Ford Ben., hawker
7 Ford John, storehouse
5 Band William, furnished apartments
3 *Void*
1 Bozward Samuel, hawker
HERE IS BRIDGE STREET; ALSO BROAD STREET

Entry for Newport Street (and North Quay) from Worcester Directory, 1912. (CMHC).

Newport Street, view from north west, April 1978. The scene includes All Saints Church bereft of its balustrading atop the tower. (CRH)

Newport Street, view from north west, 29th March 1996. A smarter scene including All Saints Church with its balustrading restored. (CRH)

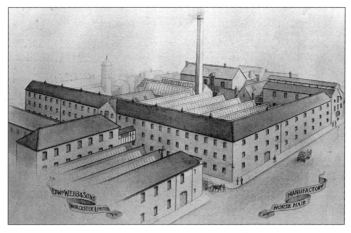

Birdport (modern Deansway) and Webb's Horse Hair Carpet Factory, c1935. The factory occupied an extensive site between Bull Entry and Copenhagen Street. Edward Webb was an enlightened employer and organised the City's first "factory school" for children in his employ. He was Mayor, 1847-8. (CMHC)

Deansway, view to the SE from All Saints Church tower, 20th July 1967. The car park, partially seen in the foreground, occupies the area now covered by the All Saints Building (phase three) of Worcester College of Technology. The City Police Station, which dates from 1939, stands between Copenhagen Street to the right and Bull Entry to the left. Left of Bull entry the "temporary building" was once the Motor Taxation Office. Left of that, the Duke of Wellington Inn. Moving left again, is the Countess of Huntingdon's Church. In the centre of the picture the rear of the Guildhall is clearly visible and on the horizon, the gas holder rises before Perry Wood. (CMH).

The same view, 7th March 1996. The Crowngate scheme has embraced the area surrounding the Huntingdon Hall and Bull Entry has been "absorbed". (CRH).

Aerial view centring on Powick Lane from the west c1925. (CRH).

Aerial view of the same area, May 1978. (CRH).

Birdport and Merryvale junction with Powick Lane, view to the north east from St. Andrews Spire (tower section) c1925. The City Rag Stores of William Prosser (est. 1860) occupied No's 22 to 28. The building to the right of the Rag Stores was once Edward Beesley's fish & chip shop and also P.J. Walley's grocery store. (TWM/WCM).

The same view in 1988. Powick Lane and the right angle into Bank Street are in the centre with the white fronted Technical College Powick Lane Annexe clearly visible. To the left is the City ambulance Station. (CRH).

The same view, 7th March 1996 with Crowngate covering the Powick Lane area. (CRH).

Bank Street with its junction to Powick Lane (left) in 1926. Norton & Whitton, confectioners were at number 16. This site was more recently occupied by Messrs Loynes the building supply merchants. (CMHC).

Chapel Walk in the Crowngate complex, view from Deansway, 3rd April 1996. The location of this walk approximates to that of the original Chapel Walk. (CRH).

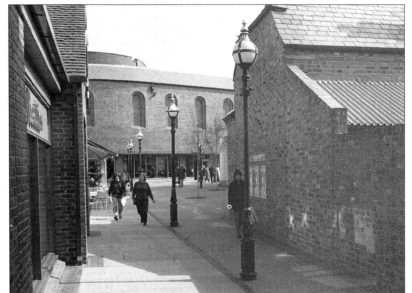

The south west corner of Bull Entry and Chapel Walk c1931 during a time of slum clearance. (ADMcG/WCM)

All Saints Church – a new vista – view from Powick Lane, 1989-90. (CRH).

Demolition of the City Ambulance Station at the north west corner of Deansway and Powick Lane, 1989-90. (CRH).

Beatties has arrived – view from a similar viewpoint, 3rd April 1996. (CRH).

The Countess of Huntingdon's Church, view from Worcester College of Technology, April 1978. The building stands in need of urgent restoration, a task in which Worcester Civic Society played a leading role. (CRH).

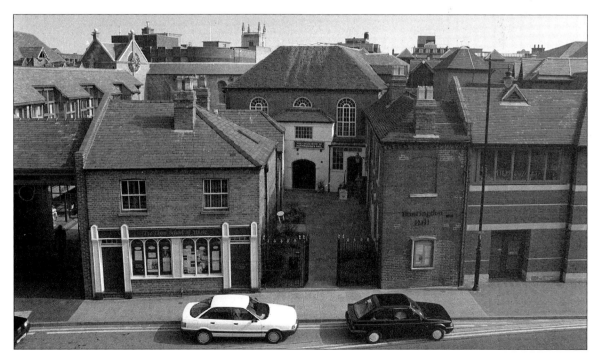

The same aspect, 3rd April 1996, also showing The Elgar School of Music. Appropriately, The Steps Cafe Bar to the right of the picture, stands upon the site of the former hostelry - The Duke of Wellington Inn. (CRH).

Group Lane, 1889. The lady on the steps is Mrs. Susan Dark. (CMHC).

Group Lane c1900. (CMHC).

Deansway, c1958. View to the south, with the Deansway Restaurant on the right-hand side. (CMHC)

Court No. 6, Quay Street, c1935 (ADMcG).

Fish Street, south side, from the west, c1900. The construction of Deansway removed most of the buildings in this picture. Fortunately, the timber-framed Farriers Arms, at the far end of this picture, is still standing. (CMHC)

2

THE GREAT WATER HIGHWAY

Looking at the steady pace of life on the River Severn today, with its pleasure craft, rowing boats, steamers and swans, it is difficult to envisage this broad expanse of water as one of the busiest water highways in Europe. In the mid-nineteenth century the Severn was a major artery for trade and the transhipment of goods from the industrial Midlands to the coast, and goods imported from the continent to the industrial heartland.

The Severn was a natural trade route, being navigable from the Bristol Channel as far inland as Bridgnorth and Shrewsbury. Until locks and weirs were added the river was tidal too – this presented problems to the shipping of the day, as the ability to pass under bridges depended upon river height. Indeed, until the arrival of steam power, the river would have presented quite a maritime aspect with the billowing of canvas and the creak and tilt of masts. As wind and tide dictated, ships, boats and barges sailing the Severn often required assistance from bow-hauliers and horses to give the necessary additional power.

The river trade developed from Roman times, through to the Middle Ages, when an assize of wine was held in the City. In the thirteenth century red and white wine was for sale at eight pence a sextar (approximately five and half pints). At this time the Prior of the monastery at Worcester stored seventy one tuns (also called "dolia") of wine in his cellar! The monastery had obtained a charter in the twelfth century granting freedom from toll for goods coming up-stream from Bristol.

Wine was certainly not the only commodity to be shipped along the Severn. Timber, grain, salt (from Droitwich), livestock and cloth had been shipped from the earliest of times and later coal and iron – including that from the Forest of Dean – joined the list together with luxury goods from the continent. With the coming of the Industrial Revolution, in the mid-eighteenth century, with its cradle in Shropshire, the river became a great export route. Naturally the City's own exports of porcelain and gloves benefited from the trade route. Worcester's fortunes as an inland port fluctuated as it vied with Tewkesbury and Gloucester to become dominant. In 1835 plans were again in prospect for Worcester to become a great inland port for seagoing vessels by making it navigable for ships of 12 feet draft, but this was defeated in Parliament when strong representation by interested parties from Gloucester exaggerated the effect of such "improvements to navigation" on Severn salmon.

In 1815, Worcester was connected to the industrial Midlands by the Worcester-Birmingham Canal, whilst further upstream, the Staffordshire and Worcestershire canal had been opened in 1770. Industry sprang up around both the riverside and canal, to take advantage of the proximity. Looking along the the canal for evidence, one finds brickworks, iron foundries, corn millers, gasworks and vinegar works plus a host of associated "service industries" – carriers and hauliers, public houses, a music hall (the Alhambra in Lowesmoor) and numerous chapels and churches to reclaim the soul.

The quaysides along the river were lively and boisterous places, with numerous warehouses and ale houses, bearing all the appearance of a small port, with sailors and boatmen looking for diversion and entertainment.

The coming of the railway to Worcester in 1850 signalled the beginning of the end for the great trade upon the Severn and the canal. Worcester sought to integrate the two enterprises with a railway line extension from Foregate Street railway station to the riverside by way of "The Butts Spur". This line looped toward Pitchcroft then headed south along the river alongside the North Quay and North Parade to pass under an archway of the bridge and so on to the South Quay, terminating at a point near where Copenhagen Street joins the Quayside. Plans were afoot to take the line to Diglis so as to enable the connection with large vessels docking there, but objections to the route by the Cathedral authorities caused the idea to be abandoned. The railway bridge over the river was opened in 1860 and connected the City to Hereford via Malvern and Ledbury.

For centuries, Worcester was the only bridging point over the Severn between Gloucester and Bridgnorth. The earliest structures were of timber, but were subject to fire and damage. The first stone bridge was built in 1313 and spanned the river, not on the site of the present City bridge, but from "Turkey" – modern day Tybridge Street – on the west bank, to Newport Street on the east. The stone bridge was fortified and carried a tower gateway with a portcullis. Responsibility for maintaining the bridge fell upon the City, a heavy responsibility as boats often crashed into it and in the seventeenth century, ice floes caused a considerable amount of damage to the structure.

Eventually, in the late eighteenth century, it was decided to replace the old stone bridge with a new structure. The position chosen was a little further downstream. On the west side a new roadway (New Road), was made and to the east, houses along Rush Alley were demolished to make way for the approach via Bridge Street. John Gwynne was the architect and designed the the graceful bridge, the basis of the one that we still see today. The new bridge was opened in 1781 and cost £29,843, a sum which included New Road and two toll houses on the west side, at the entrance to New Road.

Traffic across the bridge increased and in the nineteenth century it became necessary to widen it. This was first done in 1847 when cast iron walkways were cantilevered out at each side. Later, with the coming of the petrol engine and an increasing volume of traffic, the bridge needed to be widened and it was increased to its present width in 1932. The Prince of Wales (later Edward VIII) officially opened the bridge on 28th October that year, cutting the ribbon with a sword used by a Royalist officer at the time of The Battle of Worcester. During the widening the two charming little toll houses or "round houses" were demolished.

Recent years have seen a substantial facelift for the riverside with many unsightly areas being swept away, especially in the region of Hylton Road, Croft Road and South Parade. The Sabrina footbridge/cycleway was opened in February 1992, and now visitors can stroll in a circular route which crosses both bridges. How desirable a second footbridge would be near Diglis to complete a delightful figure of eight route for visitors and residents alike. Worcester has a glorious river frontage and should take full advantage of this natural asset.

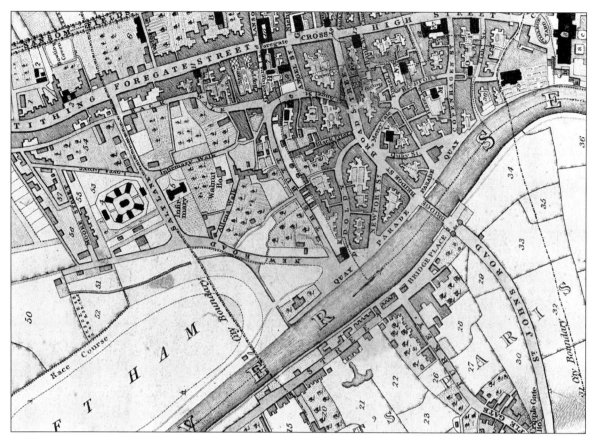

Bridge and river detail from Samuel Mainley's map of Worcester, 1822. (HWCRO).

The new bridge is seen here in this elegant engraving from Valentine Green's book about Worcester, 1796. St. Clement's church is to the far left of the picture. At the extreme left of the engraving is Worcester Royal Infirmary. (CMHC)

View to the south in the 1860's as seen from the railway bridge. Timber is stacked on the North Quay and the slipway is prominent. The Cathedral stands prior to the completion of the Victorian restoration. (CMHC).

View downstream to the south east c1880. The Butts siding spur line runs along the North Quay . To the extreme left of the scene is part of the single span bridge which carried the railway line over the slipway access to the river. On the main river bridge one of the two cantilevered footpaths (there was one on each side of the bridge) is clearly visible. (CMHC).

A closer view of the North Quay/North Parade area, c1880, showing just left of centre, the position that The Old Rectifying House now occupies. The two tall chimneys that penetrate the skyline are those of Mellor's Sauce Factory, Broad Street and Dent's Glove Factory, Copenhagen Street. (PP).

From the same viewpoint, c1900 with the timber framed Old Rectifying House pub left of centre. The name derived from the practice of "rectifying spirits", that is to say distilling them - a distillery was behind the building. Just below this popular old pub a paddle driven steamer is moored at the riverside and other steamers stretch well into the stream. (WCM).

From the same viewpoint, 5th June 1996. (CRH).

Worcester Bridge, built c1313, spanning the tidal Severn from Tybridge Street/Turkey (left) to Newport Street (right). The bridgegate at the centre span was a fortified gateway with portcullis. The heads of felons were at one time displayed here. (CMHC)

Two bridges span the river! In this rather indistinct detail from an eightenth century oil painting we can discern two bridges across the Severn. The old "Tybridge", still with its gateway, is the darker structure with a little to its right the new bridge, partially constructed and gleaming with fresh stone. Completed in 1781, it took some ten years to build and cost just under £30,000 a sum which included New Road (St. John's Road) and the two toll houses. When it came to demolish the old bridge, it was found to be surprisingly solid and gunpowder was used to destroy it! (WCM).

An entire new bridge was then begun from a design of Mr. John Gwynn, and the first stone laid by the right hon. George William earl of Coventry; to which stone is affixed a plate of copper, on which is engraved the following inscription: " Vicesimo et quinto die Julii, anno ab incarnatione, regnante Georgio tertio, prætore Edwardo Wellings, Johane Gwynn architecto, hunc primum lapidem posuit Georgius Gulielmus, comes de Coventria, huic urbi amicus patronus." After several contracts made with persons incapable of performing them, the acting commissioners found themselves unable to carry their magnificent scheme into execution without further powers, and a further toll: accordingly, in the year 1779, they applied to parliament for power to increase the tolls, and at the same time was laid a half-penny toll upon every foot passenger; this was thought very oppressive upon the labouring poor, to whom a bridge less expensive would have been equally convenient, and who had passed free from the earliest times. By the help of this additional toll the commissioners were enabled to complete the present bridge, though the avenues wait for a future day. A plan of this bridge is here engraved, which by the assistance of Mr. Gwynn we doubt not will be found very correct, and give a more exact idea than any verbal description; we shall therefore only say, it is a neat stone building of five semicircular arches springing five feet above the lowest water, the center one forty-one feet diameter, the others declining in a very small proportion, the extent from bank to bank is about 270 feet, and the width within the parapets twenty-four feet eight inches, of which a space of four feet on each side is flag paved for foot passengers, the parapets are about four feet high. Over the center arch are two tablets, one on each side, having the following inscriptions:

" The first stone of this bridge was laid by the right hon. G. W. earl of Coventry, recorder of this city, and lieutenant of the county."

" The bridge compleated in the mayoralty of Samuel Crane, esq. J. Gwynn, Archit."

The wings of the bridge are finished with a range of ballustrades extending seventy-two feet; between which and the river are lengths of flag pavements twelve feet broad, leading through arches of about five feet in width, which add to the uniformity, and are designed for towing paths, to prevent any interruption to carriages passing over the bridge. At the west end are two tollhouses, calculated more for ornament than use: it is said these houses and the gates cost near 800l. much too large a sum to be raised, for the purposes of elegance, out of the labours of the poor and the industry of the farmers. On *Sundays* a double bridge toll is paid.

The avenues when finished will in general be handsome, though I fear that which leads to the Newport-street will be steep and narrow. I could wish likewise on many accounts, that the road leading to St. John's had been made strait.

On the city side is intended an entire new street of forty feet in width, letting in a beautiful view of Malvern-hills, with the adjacent country; this, I doubt not, will render the town much healthier. On the western side the road is broad leading to St. John's, from whence to the Ludlow road will be a terrace near a mile in length, commanding a most delightful prospect of the river, bridge, town, and country round, it will never be interrupted by flood, and, if properly compleated, will certainly be one of the finest approaches to any town in England.

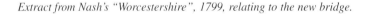

Extract from Nash's "Worcestershire", 1799, relating to the new bridge.

Sketch of the Toll Houses at the bridge end of New Road by Barribol. (WCM).

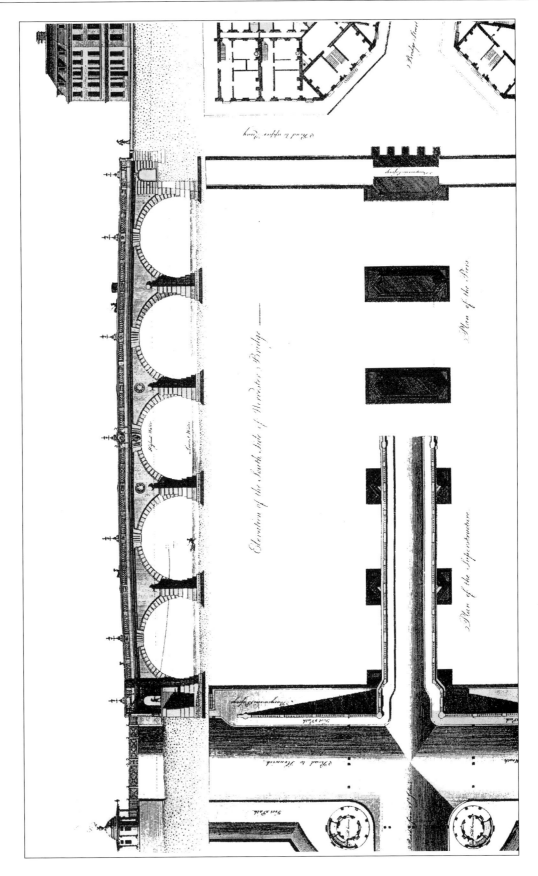

Engraving from Nash's "Worcestershire", 1799, showing the plans for John Gwynne's bridge.

ABOVE
This 19th Century engraving shows a ship's mast being lowered
to pass beneath the bridge and, to the right, men, probably bow
hauliers, pulling on a line. (CMHC).

BELOW
This centre section complete with the City Coat of Arms motif
was removed from the bridge when the 1847 extensions were
made. For many years it stood in Cripplegate Park until its
destruction by vandals in the 1980's. (CRH).

Worcester Bridge c1900 with horse tram midway. Note the absence of trees along the bank. (CMHC)

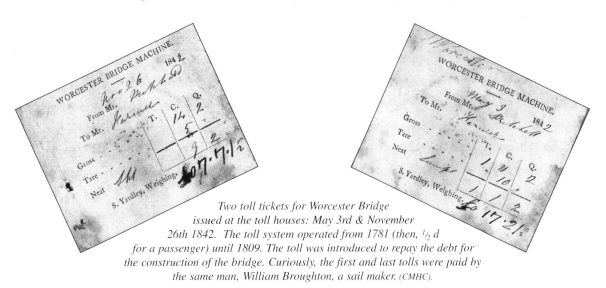

*Two toll tickets for Worcester Bridge
issued at the toll houses: May 3rd & November
26th 1842. The toll system operated from 1781 (then, $\frac{1}{2}$ d
for a passenger) until 1809. The toll was introduced to repay the debt for
the construction of the bridge. Curiously, the first and last tolls were paid by
the same man, William Broughton, a sail maker. (CMHC).*

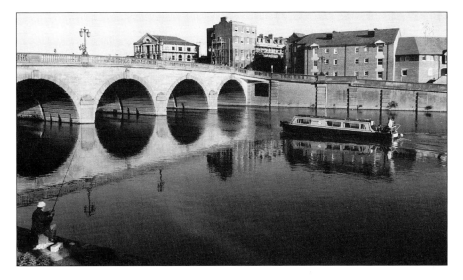

*A contrasting modern scene in 1978. Gone is the bustle of the 18th century – in 1978, leisure
is now the emphasis. (CRH).*

Just south of the present bridge in 1778 (near the present junction between Copenhagen Street and South Parade), a busy riverside scene with the smoking kilns of the porcelain factory. In the distance is Castle Hill (levelled 1823-43). The Cathedral was undergoing work (one of the slender western pinnacles is absent). Engraving: Paul Sandby 1778.

From the same viewpoint, 17th August, 1996. (CRH).

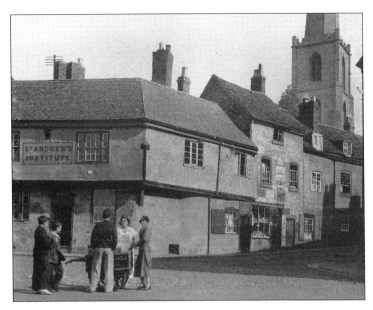

The junction of Copenhagen Street and South Quay, 1930's. St. Andrews Institute served as a social club for men and boys and also provided parish rooms. Formerly, it was the Wherry Inn. The building was demolished around 1940. Next door in Copenhagen Street is the general stores of William Jeynes. Mrs. Jeynes cut hair for ladies and children. The son, Bill Jeynes opened the fondly remembered hardware warehouse along Tybridge Street - this closed in 1985. The family business now continues in St. Johns. (WCM).

Copenhagen Street junction with South Quay, May 1959. Dent's Glove Factory still stands and the cleared site awaits further demolition before construction of the College can begin. (GNH).

Similar view, 5th June 1996. Gone are the houses. To the left, St. Andrew's Gardens and to the right, the College. (CRH).

The South Quay c1870. A busy scene with warehouses and the white fronted Wherry Inn.
The left-hand warehouse is that of J. Moore, Dealer in Marine Stores. (RJC).

More warehousing along the South Quay. Here, the "Atalanta" is moored outside Firkins & Co. (KB).

Between Warmstry Slip and the Cathedral (c1870) stood Stallard's Worcester Distillery and Bonded Vaults. (CMHC).

DENT'S GLOVES

Messrs. DENT, ALLCROFT & Co. Ltd., welcome any Visitors desirous of seeing the operations of Glove Making at their Worcester Factory, Palace Yard (adjoining the Cathedral)

The best time of the day for visiting is between 9 to 12.15 in the morning, and 2.30 to 5 in the afternoon.

Dent's advertisement, c1930.

Dents Glove Factory at the riverside 1907 - junction with Warmstry Slip to the left. Warmstry derives from Warmstry House which once stood nearby and was owned by the Warmstry family. (CMHC).

A 1920s aerial view of the eastern side of the river bordered by Bridge Street and Broad Street on the left, High Street running across the top, Copenhagen Street to the right of St. Andrew's Spire with Warmstry Slip to the far right. The course of the 1930's development of Deansway can be traced through the centre of the picture - going left to right from the broad triangle of All Hallow's (The Well), along Merryvale to its junction with Powick Lane which dog-legs up to Bank Street, then on via Birdport (thought to have derived from British Port/Gate) so to the junction with Copenhagen Street and on to Little Fish Street. Hounds Lane School stands in the centre with Group Lane to the left and Hares Lane to the right. (CMHC)

A similar vista in 1978 dominated by the austere 1960/70's architecture of Worcester College of Technology and Blackfriars shopping precinct. (CRH)

South Quay and riverside walk from the west, May 1959. The building fronting the river to the right of Dent's chimney is the site of the Porcelain Manufactury of Messrs. Flight & Barr. (GNH).

From a similar viewpoint, 5th June 1996. The area is dominated by the graceful spire of St. Andrew's, the shadow of which touches but does not soften the angular architecture of Worcester College of Technology. (CRH).

South Quay, a winter scene c1920. (CMHC).

A similar winter scene in February 1996. (CRH)

South Parade, 1967, with demolition work in progress. (CRH).

From the same viewpoint, 5th June 1996, showing the "facelift" along South Parade with Warmstry Court. (CRH).

Quay Street (once called Wooden Stair Street), and Hood Street, view from All Saint's Church tower, March 1965. The scrap yard at Hood Street was for many years a considerable eyesore. Warmstry Court now substantially covers this area. (GNH).

South Parade area in October 1969 with Worcester College of Technology, All Saint's Building, under construction. (CRH)

View up-stream from the island at Diglis, c1910. (JC).

Similar view, 5th June 1996. Still a busy scene, now with petrol storage tanks to the right. For many years Diglis was an important storage depot for fuel, with river tankers and barges pumping cargo into the many storage tanks. Most of the tanks have now been removed. (CRH).

Skating on the frozen Severn c1883. Just visible on the far side are trestle tables set out on the ice. (JC).

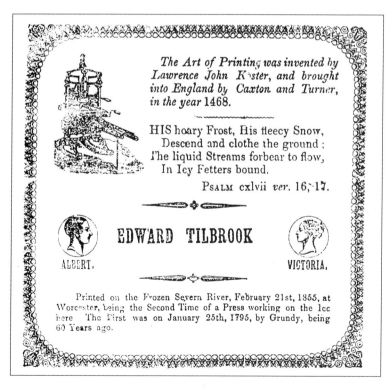

This handbill was printed on the frozen River Severn at Worcester on 21st February 1855. (CMHC).

ABOVE
The Cathedral Ferry, c1945. The ferry was a regular service for centuries between the Watergate and Paynes Meadow. Other ferries were at the Grandstand, Dog & Duck and Kepax. (CMHC).

RIGHT
The restored ferry service in the 1980's. The ferry now operates on Summer weekends and Bank Holidays. (CRH)

*Hounds Lane School is in the foreground of this March 1965 view
to the south from All Saint's Church tower. (GNH).*

Copenhagen Street, similar view to the pictures on the opposite page, 5th June 1996. (CRH)

Three views looking west down to the river progressively along Copenhagen Street, 10th March 1926 (SN) together with advertisements c1885.

ABOVE
View from the Cathedral tower to the north west, July 1969. The Power Station along Hylton Road, replaced the original station (1903) near the same site in 1942/3. Originally built to supply the City's electricity needs, it became integrated with the National Grid. (CMH).
LEFT
Demolition of the Power Station in 1979. The filling station along Hylton Road is advertising petrol at 70p per gallon for 4 star. (CMH).
BELOW
The river bridge and Power Station (note the taller chimney stacks) in February 1970 with the river in flood. (CRH).

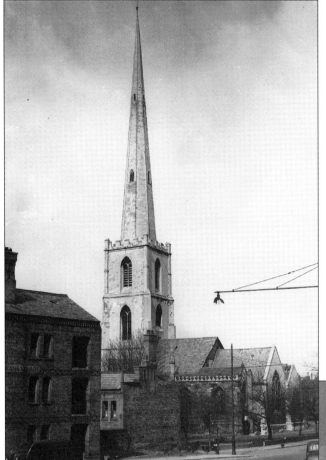

ABOVE
The junction of Copenhagen Street with Deansway c1938. St. Andrew's Church and Spire stand complete whilst to the left we can see the eastern face of St. Alban's Square. (WEN)

RIGHT
The same view, 5th June 1996. (CRH)

TOP RIGHT
The bell at St. Andrew's, still in place in the tower (March 1996). Although now silenced, once its echoing chime called across the City to summon Council members to meetings at the Guildhall. (CRH).

Bridge Street, view to the east from the bridge, c1910. An electric tram is making its way toward St. Johns. (CMHC).

From the same viewpoint, 5th June 1996. (CRH).

North Parade in 1899 complete with horse carts and a flock of sheep. Wintle's timber yard is to the centre of the picture. Note the steep gradient approaching the bridge. (CMHC).

From the same viewpoint, 5th June 1996. (CRH).

The South Parade and Butts Spur line running through the widened flood arch at the east side of the bridge An electric tram is just at the right of the bridge. c1910. (DP)

The same view, 5th June 1996. Demolition has revealed All Saint's Church to the left. (CRH)

A painting depicting the original railway bridge. The paddle boat is the "Hero". c1860. (GNH)

Hylton Road in flood, near the bridge, 1889. (DF)

The original railway bridge, spanning the river in two graceful arches c1860. Worcester was connected by railway to London in 1850 by the Oxford, Worcester & Wolverhampton line, also known as the "Old Worse and Worse Line"! Eventually this became the West Midland Railway which was then absorbed by the Great Western Railway (GWR). The bridge over the river formed an essential link as prior to its construction, passengers for Malvern and Hereford had to disembark, cross to St. Johns to take the train on from Henwick Station. The boat to the left of the bridge was the Waterman's Chapel. An old barge "The Albion" was converted for use as a chapel by the Revd. John Davies Rector of St. Clement's. (WCM).

View from the Sabrina bridge, 5th June 1996. The single span girder railway bridge replaced the double span in 1904. The centre support was retained. (CRH).

At the west end of Dolday stood the Waterman's Church. Known as "The Tin Tabernacle" it latterly became used for dances hall and roller skating. To the extreme left of the picture, the small structure is the old Albion - the original floating chapel, hauled up onto dry land. 1936, just prior to demolition. (CMHC).

Interior of the Waterman's Church at Harvest Festival. c1920. (CMHC)

Dolday, c1931, view to the east. The children are by Court No. 3 which led to Wellington Square. The All Saints Workhouse was the next building up on the left. On the distant bend is the Sow & Pigs Inn and at the end, the four windowed house is The Woolpack Inn. Dolday reached the riverside at North Quay. (ADMc/WCM).

Newport Street 'bus station in the 1940's. (GNH)

The original, mediaeval, St. Clement's Church, standing at the riverside (west) end of The Butts. Most of its parish was on the St. Johns side of the river, a short walk when the old bridge was standing. It was demolished and a new, neo-Norman church of St. Clement was built in Henwick Road, in 1823, to the design of Thomas Ingleman. (GNH)

ABOVE
Horse tram along New Road c1885. (DF).

RIGHT
Cyclist crossing the Sabrina Bridge, 5th June 1996. The bridge was opened in February 1992. Sabrina is the Latin form of the old English, Sabren, which became "Severn". In a 12th century legend, Sabrina is put to death by drowning in the river. (CRH).

BELOW
The Bathing Barge moored alongside Pitchcroft in 1891. Freshwater bathing must have been a chilly recreation in murky waters. (DF)

Hollar's engraving (1672) of the north elevation of Worcester Cathedral shows the octagonal clochium (bell tower). The clochium was demolished in 1647 for the lead of its roof which was ". . . sold for the re-edification and repair of Almshouses and churches". Note that the north transept had two windows: the single large window was added c1750 and replaced c1870. (WC).

3

CATHEDRAL AND CASTLE

For over a thousand years the skyline of Worcester has been dominated by a Cathedral dedicated to St. Mary. Before this building there were earlier churches and a cathedral in Worcester, but there is scant documentary evidence for these earliest beginnings; we are only left to conjecture – our imagination fired by the few tantalising glimpses gained through archaeology. In the post-Roman period, three church sites have been identified near the northern edge of the defensive ditch which surrounded the settlement. The churches are those of St. Helen's, St. Alban's and St. Margaret's (the latter has disappeared completely, but was in the vicinity of the western section of the car park between the College of Technology and the river).

The Hwicce (probably pronounced "Witcher"), an Anglo-Saxon tribe, occupied the Worcester area which was to become the Diocese of Worcester. During the seventh century the English Church was in a state of reorganisation and as a result, a see at Worcester was established with Bosel as its first Bishop. Bosel set to work and supervised the building of the first Cathedral, dedicated to St. Peter. Unfortunately, no physical evidence of this early building remains. In 961, Oswald, a leading cleric in the monastic reform, became Bishop. He organised the Benedictine monastic community at Worcester along more formal lines, and, to accommodate the community, built a new Cathedral, dedicated to St. Mary. This new Cathedral was completed in 983.

Following the Norman Conquest in 1066, Wulfstan, a Saxon bishop, remained in office throughout that turbulent period. He had been Prior at Worcester at the time of attacks by the Danes during which the Cathedral had been sacked. The number of monks had dropped to only twelve by the time Wulfstan became Bishop in 1062, and he set about restoring the community and replacing the badly damaged church. Described as a man of striking personality and genuine piety, he soon had a community of fifty monks, and by 1084, had started work on a new cathedral church. Within five years the monks had moved into the new Cathedral.

As Wulfstan ordered the church of Oswald to be unroofed and destroyed, it is probable that it stood in the building line of the new Cathedral's nave and cloister. It is also probable that fragments from Oswald's Saxon Cathedral were, where useful, incorporated into the new building. These Saxon fragments can be seen in the cloisters and the vaulting of the undercroft, adjacent to the dormitory ruins. Wulfstan's new Cathedral was built from pale Cotswold limestone and green Highley sandstone. The design was simple and spacious, whitewashed inside and out. The crypt, with its ambulatory, side chapels and apsidal east end, is the most evident survivor from this early period The finest remaining Norman crypt in the country, its great sinews of masonry reach out to form the vaulting, giving an impression of strength and serenity.

It had long been thought that the shrines of both St. Oswald and St. Wulfstan were in the crypt, but research can find no evidence for this and archaeology supports this view, as the floor of its ambulatory does not exhibit the sort of wear one would expect from the passage of the thousands of pilgrims who would have paid homage there. Remains indicate that the extent of Wulfstan's building was as wide as the Cathedral today, the nave being the same length, with the tower and north and south transepts being of equal area to those that now stand.

Over the course of the next two hundred years, the Cathedral continued to evolve under the care of successive Bishops, master masons and craftsmen, reflecting transitions in fashion and architectural style. The Benedictine Order were in occupation for some six hundred years at the Cathedral, until the Dissolution in the reign of Henry VIII. The requirements of monastic life necessarily had a great influence upon the building's design. The Chapter House, where the monks conducted their day-to-day business, dates from around 1110, and is the earliest example of a completely circular chapter house – the vaulting springing from a single central column. This circular design was later emulated at Lincoln and Wells. Outside the Chapter House in the cloisters, monks sat at desks, working on manuscripts. The slots, or "squints" in the masonry adjacent to the windows were incorporated to give an easy, "at a glance" view to ensure that all monks were working at their tasks. Deep recesses in the cloister walls probably held the cupboards where the monks' books were stored and their washing trough or lavatorium, which was supplied with fresh water. To the east of the cloisters were added an infirmary and reredorter, but little now remains. The monastic refectory, now called College Hall, is part of the complex of buildings used by the Kings School. Here the monks would have eaten in silence whilst listening to readings. At the east end is a carving of Christ in Majesty. This powerful, seated figure is thought to have inspired Graham Sutherland in designing his great tapestry for Coventry Cathedral. As recently as 1861 the 14th century monastic Guesten Hall stood to the east of College Hall. One wall is all that remains of the Hall which, in monastic times, provided rest and refreshment for travellers. The magnificent timber roof, which once graced the Guesten Hall, was preserved and can be seen at the Avoncroft Museum of Buildings near Bromsgrove.

Nearby is the ancient Edgar Tower. The gateway, once known as St. Mary's Gate, has its origins in the mid-14th Century. Above the eastern arch, King Edgar, St. Oswald, St. Wulstan, Bosel, Ethelred, Osric and Florence gaze down on those who pass beneath. The current set of figures dates from 1910, following the major Victorian restoration of the Cathedral in 1857-74. The Water Gate, constructed in 1378, was stoutly built with inner and outer archways and a portcullis. Cargoes arriving at high tide could be unloaded there in safety.

Returning now to the Cathedral, mention must be made of the nave with its beautiful west window, rich with images of the creation, made by the Birmingham firm of Hardman (1863-65). Looking from the nave one can appreciate the Quire, with at its eastern end, the high altar and reredos, the work of Sir George Gilbert Scott, (c1870). Beyond the Quire, soaring pillars of Purbeck marble draw the gaze upwards to the splendours of the Lady Chapel ceiling superbly painted by Hardman (c1870). It depicts numerous saints amid elegant swirls of floral patterns. The focal point is the sanctus design, with the figure of Christ on the central boss.

Situated in front of the high altar is the tomb of King John, who died in 1216 aged 48. In a codicil to his will he ordered that he should be buried in Worcester Cathedral. His tomb bears the Purbeck marble effigies of the King and the two Worcester saints, Wulstan, (who was his patron saint) and Oswald. The Cathedral, already a place of pilgrimage for those visiting the shrines of Oswald and Wulfstan, attracted additional revenue as the resting place of a king.

Another royal connection is that of Prince Arthur's Chantry, which stands to the south of the high altar The tomb contains the remains of the fifteen year-old prince, who, but for his untimely death at Ludlow two months after his marriage to Catherine of Aragon in 1502, would have become King of England. Its interesting to speculate on how different our history would have been if Arthur's younger brother, Henry, had not become King Henry VIII and married his late brother's widow, Catherine of Aragon. The Chantry, built in 1504, is richly decorated. The outer wall has many heraldic statues and symbols, while inside, the vaulted ceiling has graceful stone pendants. The stone figures of the reredos suffered severely at the hands of over zealous Kings Commissioners who regarded such figures as idolatrous. The Commissioners were acting on behalf of Edward VI, the tragically short-lived son of Henry VIII. For all the ravages caused by the Dissolution of the Monasteries and the changes brought about by the Reformation, Worcester gained an educational institution in the form of the Kings School founded by Henry VIII in 1541. This school not only has a high reputation for its scholarship, but it also provides choristers for the Cathedral choir.

The Cathedral Library holds a famous collection of mediaeval literature which includes many important musical manuscripts, amongst them, "The Antiphoner" which is the earliest existing manuscript containing the complete services of the Benedictine Order in the 13th century. "The Worcester Fragments", another important set of pre-14th century manuscripts, provide evidence that the Worcester school of musical learning was second to none in the Christian world. These manuscripts contain some of the earliest known forms of polyphonic choral writing.

In this section of the book one can scarcely do justice to the magnificence that is Worcester Cathedral – it warrants a complete volume.

The Cathedral from the north east, an engraving from Wild's book of Worcester Cathedral, 1823. Elegant pinnacles, added around 1712, soar into the sky and the whole scene is romanticised by the omission of Old St. Michael's Church and cottages, which stood at the north east corner of the Cathedral. The slender pinnacles were subject to damage and frequently in need of repair. Eventually they were removed altogether, together with the eastern flying buttresses, during the Victorian restoration. (CMHC).

The Cathedral with the medieval church of Old St. Michael's clearly shown. The church was demolished in 1840. (WCM).

The north eastern aspect c1880. Note that the flying buttresses at the east end of the Lady Chapel have been removed and that the tower is more ornately decorated. (WCM).

The Cathedral from the north east, seen from the lower roof of the Giffard Hotel, 1978. (CRH).

View from the north west prior to the installation of Perkins' Rose Window (1863-65).   (WC).

The Cathedral Choir, 1909.   (CMHC)

Distribution of "The Bread Dole" inside the Chapter House, 1909. (CMHC).

Church Army wagon outside the Cathedral, c1910. (CMHC)

The nave, view to the west, with its simple and elegant tierceron vaulting (c1377). 1984 (CRH).

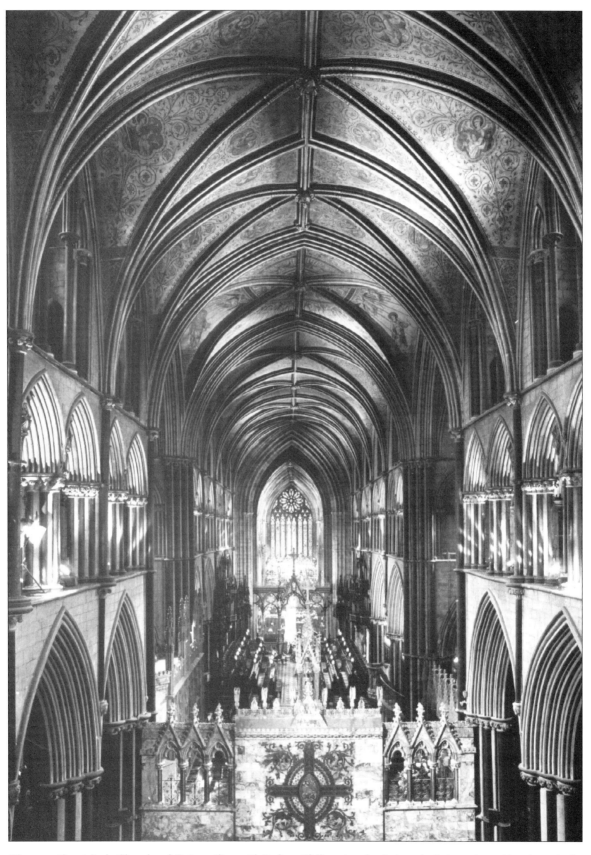

The magnificent Lady Chapel and Quire ceiling with its beautifully restored paintings depicting saints. Also shown is the sanctus design encircling the central boss with its carving of Christ. View from the east end, 1984 (CRH).

TOP
*The Guesten Hall, north east side, c1860, in a poor
state of repair with the roof structure exposed. (WC).*
ABOVE
*The remaining (east) wall of the Guesten Hall, 1978.
This view shows what would have been the interior
surface of the wall. (CRH).*
LEFT
*The interior of the Guesten Hall: drawing (1861)
showing how it would have looked if restored.
Unfortunately the fight was lost and the hall was
demolished (1862) with exception of the east wall,
which still stands. The superb roof structure was re-
used with some modifications, in the building of Holy
Trinity Church, Shrub Hill Road. When Holy Trinity
was demolished, the fine roof was saved and is now to
be seen at Avoncroft Museum of Buildings, near
Bromsgrove. (CMHC).*

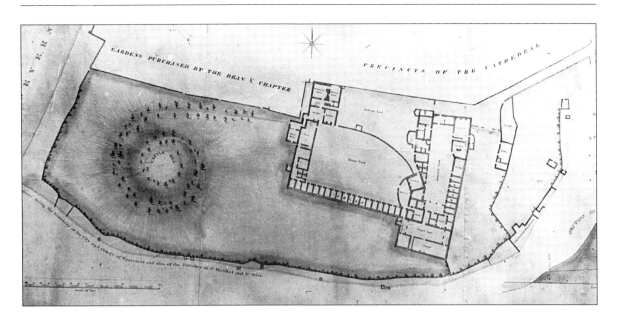

Plan of Castle Hill, November 1822, by Samuel Mainley. Urse d'Abitot, Sheriff of Worcester, built the motte and bailey mound in 1069. Later it was reinforced with stone. For centuries some of the sturdy buildings at the base of Castle Hill served as one of the City gaols. The site today is in the riverside gardens of the Kings School. (WC).

Castle Hill, which stood 25 metres high, once played an important role in the defences of the City, particularly during the mid-12th century war between King Stephen and Matilda and again during the Battle of Worcester. It met an ignominious end when Thomas Eaton, a local bookseller and antiquary, bought the hill in 1814 and demolished it between 1823 and 1843 for gravel and "antiquarian finds". The sketch shows men at digging and sieving the rubble in 1826. A neolithic socketed axe and numerous Roman coins were discovered beneath the hill. (WC).

The Edgar Tower, east side, an engraving from Laird's book about Worcester, 1810. The windows to the left were those of the Registrar's office. (CMHC).

The Bishops Palace (just off modern Deansway), an engraving from Valentine Green's book of Worcester, 1796. The Palace dates from the time of Bishop Godfrey Giffard (one time Chancellor of England). Giffard became Bishop of Worcester in 1268 and almost immediately commenced the building of his residence. The rib-vaulted "Abbott's Kitchen" dates from this time. Royal visits to the Palace, include those of Elizabeth I, James II, Charles I and George III. The Palace continued as the Bishop's residence until 1846; it then became The Deanery and served as such until 1941. It now houses diocesan offices.

CENTRE PICTURE
Edgar Tower, the gateway to the monastery at Worcester, seen here about 1880, dates from the mid 14th century. The massive wooden doors are original, thankfully having escaped 19th century restoration work when masonry and some windows were replaced. The statues illustrated here were placed in the niches above the gateway in 1910. (DF).

STATUES, CLOCKWISE FROM TOP LEFT
BOSEL, Bishop of the Hwiccian's AD 679-692; ST. OSWALD, Bishop of Worcester, AD 961-992; KING EDGAR, King of England AD 959-975, benefactor to the Priory at Worcester; OSWALD SUBREGULUS, Sub-king of the Hwiccians and joint founder of the Bishopric; ETHELRED REX, King of Mercia, AD 679-708, founder of the Bishopric; FLORENCE OF WORCESTER, historian, died AD 1118; WINSIN, first prior at the monastery, AD 971-992; ETHELRED DUX, Duke of Mercia, AD c880-911 and ETHELFLAEDA, daughter of King Alfred, wife of Ethelred AD c885-918; ST. WULFSTAN, born AD 1008, monk, 1037, successively master of the school, precentor and treasurer and prior c1052, Bishop, 1062-1095; WERNFRITH, Bishop of Worcester, AD 873-915.

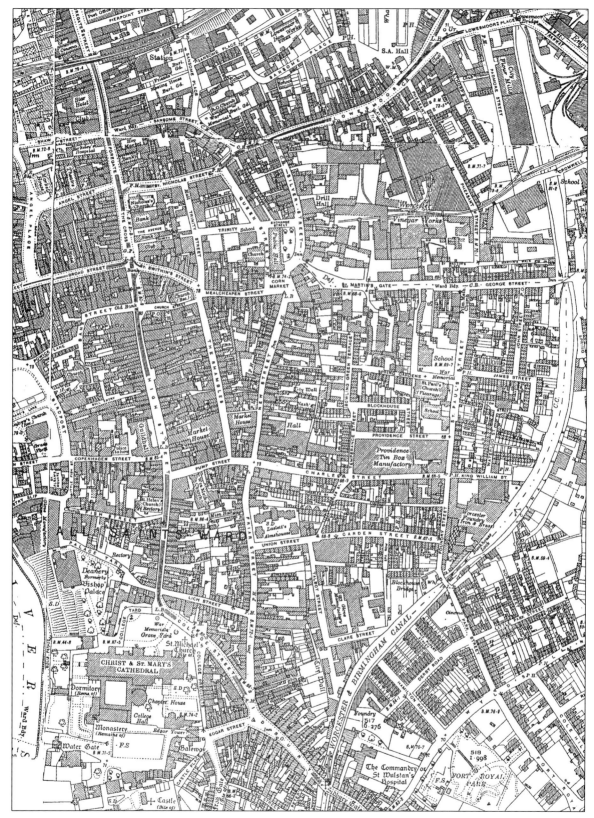

Detail from Samuel Mainley's map of Worcester, 1822. (HWCRO).

4

THE PATTERN OF THE PAST – THE FOREGATE TO SIDBURY

The central area from Foregate to Sidbury has traditionally been the commercial hub of the City. The market day hurly-burly as cattle, produce and locally-made goods arrived would all have combined to assail the senses with a riotous cascade of sounds, colours, cries and smells. Here, too, in the early 1900s, horse-drawn carriages competed with trams, and cyclists weaved between them all, taking care to avoid locking their wheels into the tram lines!

Reaching above the City skyline, church towers and steeples stretch into the sky as they have for centuries, providing excellent points of reference when tracing building lines and the relationship of streets. Standing proudly at The Cross is the tiered and cupola-topped tower of St. Nicholas. This restrained English baroque edifice dates from the early 1730s when it replaced the 12th century church on this site. It is the work of Georgian architect, Humphrey Hollins. Like so many City centre churches, St. Nicholas had been redundant for many years, its parish of closely knit houses having been reduced over the years by successive clearances and the proliferation of commercial interests, notably banks, offices and shops. It is now Pepper's Restaurant.

Three other Georgian churches grace the skyline, those of All Saints, Bridge Street, possibly the work of Richard Squire, (1742); St. Swithin's, Church Street, Thomas & Edward Woodward, (1736), and St. Martins, The Cornmarket, Anthony Keck, (1772). All Saints and St. Martins continue to be used for worship, while St. Swithin's stands redundant, although restored and under the protective wing of the Redundant Churches Fund.

In High Street stands The Guildhall, one of the finest buildings of its kind in the country. The original Guildhall on this site was established to house medieval guilds following the Charter granted to the City by Henry III in 1227. The present building was opened in 1724, with north and south wings added in 1725 and 1727 respectively. The cost of the building was around £4,000. The statue of Queen Anne, now in the niche above the main entrance, once stood outside the front door of the previous Guildhall. At either side of the main door stand statues of King Charles I and King Charles II, whilst above the portal, a life size head of "Old Nick" or as some say, Oliver Cromwell, hangs, pinned back by the ears. Looking higher up one sees the glorious blaze of Thomas White's carved and painted pediment, a fanfare in stone to the Hanovarians whose arms are displayed. A glance at the roofline reveals a group of classical allegorical figures representing Justice, Plenty, Peace, Chastisement and Labour. Inside, the upper floor accommodates the superbly elegant 110 feet long Assembly Room, which, with its Adam style detailing, is another of the building's splendours.

In the nineteenth century the City was unusual for having within its walls both a Cornmarket and a Corn Exchange. The two cornmarkets were the result of an argument between opposing political factions during the depression that followed the end of the Napoleonic Wars and the highly contentious Corn Laws. A race to complete the rival buildings ensued. In the event, the Cornmarket, the traditional site for corn dealing, lost the contest to the the group who sought to retain the protectionism of the Corn Laws (largely farmers and hoteliers, innkeepers and businessmen from the Foregate area all motivated by self interest). The pilastered Corn Exchange, standing in Angel Street at the northern entrance to Angel Passage, was opened in 1848.

The 'Cornmarket', never serving in that capacity, became home for a succession of ventures, including those of a music hall. It was later known as the Public Hall. During its time it resounded to performances by Sir Edward Elgar, Jenny Lind, Dvorak and John Philip Souza. It was the scene of many a stormy election meeting and even housed a popular roller skating rink. During World War II it became a British Serviceman's Club and it continued as a Public Hall until becoming a bingo club, The Majestic. Finally it was demolished to make way for the City Walls Road. The space is now a car park. Since the Public Hall's demolition, Worcester has been sadly in need of a public hall to take its place. Its rival, the Corn Exchange, survived for a while as a centre for corn dealing, but it too, in its turn, was used for a variety of other enterprises including boxing, auction sales and cage bird shows. Standing abandoned and empty for many years it eventually became absorbed into the scheme which included Angel Passage.

Friar Street and its continuation into New Street provide the greatest concentration of timber framed buildings in the City. The street was originally a back lane that afforded access to the properties in High Street, but with arrival of the Franciscan Friars (or "greyfriars" after the colour of their habit) and the founding of their friary in the street in 1235, the way became of greater importance. The friary was adjacent to the City Wall, and its associated church, dedicated to St Lawrence, was just outside the wall. The church was demolished in 1538, the site being occupied much later by Sigley's Sweet Factory in Carden Street. The outstanding building in Friar Street is the house called The Greyfriars which was built in the late 1400s by Thomas Green, a wealthy brewer and innkeeper. The property had a succession of owners and was used for multitude of purposes. The passage through the gateway of Greyfriars led to George's Yard, a court with ten dwellings named after the George family, who occupied part of Greyfriars from 1724 to 1841. Eventually the building became very dilapidated and was bought by Mr. Matley Moore and his sister Elsie. Between the 1940s and the early 1970s they lovingly restored the building and created the charming garden at the back of Greyfriars. The National Trust now has charge of the property.

Other important buildings in Friar Street include numbers 40 to 42, a four bay building, built around 1600 as three clothiers' houses. Known as Tudor House, it now houses the Museum of Local Life, but in its long history it has been a dwelling house, The Cross Keys Inn, The Tudor Coffee House and the Administrative Centre for the City Education Authority. Another important building is presently occupied by Heroes Restaurant, and dates from around 1600. Records show that in 1614, Francis Hughes, who was both a brewer and a surgeon, lived here.

At the corner of Friar Street and Union Street stand the deceptively ancient-looking Laslett's Alms Houses. It surprises many to discover that these half-timbered buildings were built in 1912 in the Tudor style by William Laslett, a wealthy and eccentric local benefactor. Prior to their construction, the City Gaol, complete with treadmill and cells for some 40 prisoners, occupied this corner site. When in 1867, the City and County Gaols combined at Castle Street, William Laslett bought the Union Street site for £2,250 and developed it for use as almshouses.

Almost every property in Friar Street has a fascinating history, but regretably space only permits a few examples to be described. New Street has a similar pedigree. To give a flavour of the occupancy of Friar Street, two extracts from street directories are included on page 130: Littlebury's 1912 and Kelly's 1928.

The Cross, view to the north in the 1880's. Horse tram lines are in evidence and a tram is just discernible at the crossroads with The Foregate. St. Nicholas Church towers into the sky above neighbouring buildings. The original church upon this site included a "cell" for an anchorite - a religious hermit. Next to the church the building, now Lloyds Bank was in the 1800s "Worcester Bank". It stands four square and is an excellent example of Victorian neoclassical architecture. Designed by E. W. Elmslie, it dates from 1862 when it replaced St. Nicholas' rectory. Next to the bank, this side of The Avenue, is The Golden Cross, a "Clothing Establishment" according to the legend above the first floor windows. The site became The National Provincial Bank and after other banking occupancies is now a branch of the Halifax Building Society. (CMHC).

From a similar viewpoint, 18th July 1996. (CRH).

The junction of The Cross and St. Swithin's Street, c1876. The line of properties to the right of The Civet Cat along the north side of St. Swithin's Street was demolished for widening which took place in 1878. "Lot 1" can be seen upon the side of the corner building. The curiously named Civet Cat was the premises of G. Birley, jeweller and silversmith (Later Cassidy's). A civet, incidentally, is a species of cat which exudes a strong, musky perfume. (WCM).

From a similar viewpoint, 18th July 1996. Following the 1880s re-development of the corner and the north side of St. Swithin's Street, the corner site was a grocers for many years, J.J Williams & Co in 1912 and later The International Stores. It is now occupied by The National Westminster Bank. (CRH).

The Cross, view from the north, c1920, with an electric tram destined for Barbourne. (ECH).

The west side of The Cross, c1935. The Maypole Dairy Co. is currently Worcester College of Technology's "Learning Shop"; Stewart's is Cancer Research and H. Samuel stands vacant. (RN-J/MH).

J. W. CASSIDY & SON Ltd.
64 High Street,
: WORCESTER :
Greenwich Time Daily by Wireless.
And at 12 Gt. Western Arcade, BIRMINGHAM.   Phone Cent 6735.

SOUVENIR SPOONS in several varieties

Up-to-date Stock of all kinds of JEWELLERY, etc.
Ladies' Leather Hand Bags.   Special English Goods.
Phone 1038.

ABOVE LEFT
High Street in festive mood in the 1880s. The area at the right-hand side approximates to that where Woolworths and Marks & Spencer stand today. There is not a bare head in this scene.   (AJB).
ABOVE RIGHT
Cassidy's jewellery shop at 64, High Street, as seen in an advertisement, c1930. (CMHC).

Flags again with High Street decked out for the coronation of George VI in 1937. Nearest to the right-hand edge is Hill's Famous Boots shop, next door to that, Hunt's, with their prominent sign "Noted for Severn Salmon". Two doors down from Hunt's was Marks & Spencer and next door to that, F.W. Woolworth & Co. (RJC).

High Street, view to the Cross, c1910. At the corner of Bank Street (off to the left) is The Capital & Counties Bank (Old Bank building). The clock is above Birley & Co (ex Civet Cat), later Cassidy's Jewellers. (GNH).

High Street, September 1944. Simes Department Store at the corner of Bank Street became Bobby's and now is Debenhams. (JPF).

The west side of High Street c1920. It is difficult to discern exactly what each of the businesses were but the 1928 Kelly's Directory provides the information. For comparison, the present (1996) occupant is shown in brackets:- Left to right, William Rayner, Furrier, (Next); "Twells", Ladies Hairdressers (Salisburys); Kate Rowe, Servants Registry Office (New Look); Johnson Brothers, Dyers (Granada); W. W. Spicer, Shakespeare Cafe (Our Price Music/Records); Jas. Lucking & Co., Opticians (Card Warehouse); Henry Playfair Ltd., Boot & Shoe Manufactures (Radio Rentals); Downs & Willes, Outfitters (Bookshops); George Oliver, Boot Maker (Boots & Co). Newspaper offices and the department store of Simes complete the run to Bank Street, (this section is now Debenhams store). (CMHC).

From a similar viewpoint, 19th July 1996, with shady trees and pedestrianisation. (CRH).

View down the High Street, c1930. To the right was W&F Webb & Co., furnishers, next, The White Tea Rooms, then Whitts, general drapers, milliners and underwear specialists. The area of Whitts is now occupied by Littlewoods store.   (CMHC).

From a similar viewpoint, 19th July 1996. (CRH).

High Street corner with Bank Street (to the right), view to the south during 1940's. Clearly visible at the junction is Simes department store, now Debenhams. On the left of the street is David Greig, grocers and next to that Shuter & Flays grocery store. (CMHC)

From a similar viewpoint, 18th July 1996. (CRH).

Two pictures of "The Electric Tramway Siege" when for two years, 1903-04, the City centre was in chaos as the horse tram lines were replaced by the more extensive electric tramway system. The trams remained in service until 1928. Right: Broad Street; below: The Cross. (CMHC)

Bank Street, view to the east, c1958. (GNH)

Bank Street, view to the west, c1958. The Berkeley Arms Inn is at the far end. (GNH)

The Guildhall (Valentine Green engraving, 1796). The building dates from 1721 but the function of a "Guild Hall" dates from the granting of a charter to the citizens of Worcester in 1227, when, with other privileges, Henry III permitted a Guild of Merchants to be established to control trade within the City.

The Guildhall with a Worcester Young Farmers carnival float, c1950. (HWCRO).

ABOVE: Bradburn's Doll's Hospital shop, 101, High Street, September 1938. Bradburn's were also musical instrument, radio, TV and toy dealers. The business occupied these premises from the 1920's until closure in December 1957. Previously it had been "Celia House", the Fine Art and Music Warehouse of Walter Harris, who was also a photographer, (1912 Directory). (CMHC).

RIGHT: The Worcester Toy Shop - "Doll's Hospital". Advert c1930. (CMHC).

THE

Worcester Toy Shop

(Mrs. A. M. BRADBURN).

101 High Street

(near Cathedral).

Here you will always find a delightful and extensive stock of high-class

Toys, Dolls, Games, Meccano and Hornby, Books, Leather and Fancy Gifts, Necklaces, etc.

Speciality :—**DOLLS' HOSPITAL.**

LEFT
Lich Street, c1900. This timber framed building was once called "The Deanery", but no such usage is recorded. It was swept away with the entire street during the massive re-development of the area during the mid 1960s. The loss of this street and the historic Lich Gate was largely responsible for the "Rape of Worcester" charge in the architectural and national press. The area is now covered by the Giffard Hotel complex and the concrete car park that intrudes into Friar Street. (CMHC).

BELOW
The Lich Gate. Ye Olde Punch Bowl Inn can be seen at the College Street side of the gateway. The Lich Gate provided a resting place for coffins as they entered the Cathedral graveyard. Lich Street was a principal way into the City connecting Sidbury to High Street, by a "dog leg" route. The construction of College Street cut the corner off. (CMHC).

The southern end of High Street, c1912. The Elgar music and pianoforte shop was nearby on the left (number 10, just out of sight). Number 6 is William Leicester JP, Printer & Stationer; 5, Frederick Lightowler, Tobacconist; 4, "Ye Olde Glove Shoppe" was run by Mrs. Sarah Adams. (CMHC).

The southern end of the High Street from a similar viewpoint, 18th July 1996. (CRH).

TOP
View along Sidbury (west side), from the south west, to the junction of Lich Street (left) and Friar Street (ahead) c1920. This section today is all known as Friar Street and dominated by the architecture of the 1960s multi-storey car park. Nearest on the left is Hall's, Silversmith, next at 1, Sidbury, McCowan's "Bazaar", across Lich Street at 64, Friar Street is McCowan's leather goods shop (JMcC).
ABOVE
The same view, 17th August 1996. (CRH).
LEFT
An upstairs room at McCowan's leather shop with J.T. and J.C. McCowan and Violet McCowan. Violet later had a household stores shop at 15, Sidbury, whilst J.C. had a fishing tackle shop at 8, Silver St. c1922 (JMcC).

ABOVE LEFT
College Street, c1880. All the buildings in this scene have vanished. New St. Michael's Church, built in 1839 replaced the mediaeval, church of "old" St. Michael which stood near the south eastern corner of the Cathedral. Old St. Michael's was demolished in 1840. New St. Michael's was closed in 1907 and later became a Diocesan Registry and store. It was demolished in 1962. To the right of the church is the shop of Henry Handley, Violin Maker. The Giffard Hotel, flats and car park now occupy the site. Note the drinking fountain complete with chained drinking vessel set into the Cathedral perimeter wall. (CMHC).

INSET (ABOVE RIGHT)
Henry Handley, working in his shop between St. Michael's Church and the Lich Gate. He was born in 1839 and after making 105 violins and 10 violas, retired in 1927. He died in 1931. (CMHC).

BELOW
The Giffard area, 17th August 1996, from the same viewpoint (note the same wall in the left foreground). (CRH).

LEFT
View of Lich Street area from the Cathedral tower, c1957. The small stone walled garden with a large scale tourist information map of Worcester occupied the cleared area until re-development. (CMHC).

BELOW
The cleared area at the north east end of High Street in 1965 (CMH).

ABOVE
The north east end of High Street, 17th August 1996. (CRH)

LEFT
Demolishing the north west corner of College Street, where it joins Lich Street, 1st June 1951. (N).

BELOW
The same view, 19th July 1996 (CRH)

The junction of St. Nicholas Street and The Foregate c1870 with J & W Badger's Ironmongers store at the corner and to the right, The Hollybush Inn. The corner site was re-developed along with the eastern side of The Foregate in a flourish of terracotta in 1900. (CMHC).

The same aspect, 18th July 1996. (CRH).

The corner of Angel Street and The Foregate, July 1939. Barnett's clothing shop at the corner with England's Shoes next door and W.H. Smiths next along in The Foregate. (JPF).

From the same viewpoint, 23rd August, 1996. (CRH).

ABOVE

The Shambles in the late 1940's, view from the north, with J & F Hall's ironmongers shop at the corner of Church Street. On the opposite corner, the junction with Mealcheapen Street, is Foss's Corn & Seed Merchants shop. "Shambles" derives from "flesh-shambles," – benches for cutting and selling meat. For decades there was a high concentration of butchers and fishmongers: the 1928 Directory for Butchers' Market (from Shambles to New St.) lists some twenty one butchers. (CMHC)

LEFT

The Shambles, corner with Church Street (once, Dish Market) with Hall's Ironmongers shop, October 1961, just prior to closure and demolition. (GNH)

BELOW

A similar view, 18th July 1996. The Shambles character has changed: now the street contains shops that reflect the present trends in "consumerism" with electrical goods and discount stores, sports, clothing and shoe shops. Hall's has gone – replaced by a concrete structure (H. Samuel). Some aspects remain: Pratley's china shop with it's piles of plates and pinnacles of porcelain, some fruit and vegetable shops and the Market Hall for small traders. (CRH).

The Shambles, view from the south, c1905. To the left is the Butchers Arms and, to the right of the picture, a butchers shop complete with meat on benches. (CMHC).

St Swithin's Church, revealed following the demolition of Hall's ironmongers shop at the corner of The Shambles and Church Street in the mid 1960's. This Georgian church dates from 1736 and is the work of Thomas & Edward Woodward. Hardy's furniture store is to the left; this well-known shop ran through to St. Swithin's Street and was previously the premises of the Arcade Cinema. (CMHC).

SHAMBLES.
From St. Swithin's st. to Pump st.

West side.

1 & 2 **HALL J. & F. LIMITED,** builders' merchants, ironmongers, hot water engineers & fencing mfrs
3 Bozward Wm. fruitr
4 Ward Ernest, butcher
5, 6, 7 & 8 Webb W. & F. Ltd. house furnishers
9 Taylor Harry Thos.btchr
10 Andrews Claude H.btchr
11 Andrews Walt.W.butchr
12 Thompson Jn. G.greengro
13 Andrews Lawrence Walt. butcher
15 Shapland Sid, fishmngr
Butchers' Arms P.H. Thos. Betteridge
..here is Shambles entry..
16a, Winkle S. J. & Sons, china dlrs
17, 18 & 19 Elt Albt. bootma
..entrance to Market hall..
19a, Smith R. J. butcher
Coach & Horses P.H. Jn. Bertram Shepherd

21 Potter Wm. Hy. butcher
22 Embling Benj. confctnr

.....here is Pump st.....

East side.

25 Sallis Edwd. Hy. provsn. dlr
27 Maggs Rt. Wm. boot dlr
28 Lennards Ltd. boot mkrs
29 Maggs Ltd. clothiers
..entrance to Market hall..
....here is Market pass....
30 Pearks' Dairies Ltd. gros
31 Millis Edwd. T. fish fryer
32 Maypole Dairy Co. Ltd
33 Thompson Wm. fishmngr
34 Star Tea Co. Ltd. grocers
35 Smith Sidney, pork btchr
36 Smith Alfd. confctnr
37 Till Chas. butcher
38 Lydford Albt. tripe dlr
39 Tyler Herbt. & Harvey, butchers
40 Andrews J. M. butcher
41 Liverpool Vaults, Chas. Worley
42 Baker Mrs. Jane,greengro
43 Thompson Jack, fishmngr
44 Mason George J. Ltd. grocers
45 Philpott Fredk. butcher
46 & 46a, Sargent Mrs. Edith Maud, butcher
47 Till Mrs. Mary, butcher
48 Smith Wm. butcher
49 Blackburn Fredk. Jas. butcher
50 Harris Clarence, butcher
51 Marshall Mrs. E. boot dlr
52 Marshall Herbt. clothier

FRIAR STREET.

33 & 35 Hodges John Albert, *Globe Vaults*
31 Chamberlain Wm., *Coventry Arms Inn*
29 Thomas James Alfred, baker
27 Braithwaite James, cabinet maker and furniture dealer
HERE IS COURT NO. 3
Friar Street Mission Room—Services—Sunday, 6.30 p.m.; Band of Hope, Monday, 6.30 p.m.: Thursday, 7.30 p.m.—C. Cockbill, *Missioner*
Wyatt's Almshouses
25 Evans H. & Co., lamp and oil stores
23 Lawrence Sidney Frank, boot and shoe maker
HERE IS COURT NO. 4
21 Thompson Mrs. Mary, fruiterer
19 Branch of Tudor Coffee House, Ernest Wood, *Manager*
HERE IS COURT NO. 5
17 Sheppy Charles, grocer and tea dealer
HERE IS UNION STREET
Laslett Almshouses, in course of erection
15 Frost Thomas, general dealer
13 Waldron Henry, china rivetter
HERE IS COURT NO. 6 (GEORGE'S YARD)
George's Yard—
,, (1) Rowberry William, labourer
,, (2) Blair George, labourer
,, (3) Croft William, carpenter
,, (4) *Void*
,, (5) Rodber William, glover
,, (6) Smith George, labourer
,, (7) Bunn Mrs. Emma, lodgings
,, (8) *Void*
,, (9) *Void*
,, (10) Allen James Wm., carpet weaver
,, (11) Diaper Miss Alice
,, (12) Ranford Edward, glover
11 Hale Ernest, fruiterer
9 Goodwin Edward J., working tinsmith
7 Rowberry William, fried fish shop
5 *Ye Old City Bakery*—Wall Charles Alfred, baker, &c.
3 Fidler John, picture frame dealer, &c.
1 Herberts (Herbert John Tasker),drapers
HERE ARE CHARLES STREET AND NEW STREET; ALSO PUMP STREET
RETURN
2 Seymour William, *Eagle Vaults*
4 Evans William, shopkeeper
6 Gardiner George, boot and shoe repairer
HERE IS COURT NO. 9
8 Annetts and Newman, shopkeepers
10 Inchard Henry, hairdresser
12 Frost Thomas, wardrobe dealer
14 Taylor Herbert, general dealer
HERE IS COURT NO. 10
16 Hughes William, butcher
18 Giles Ernest, watchmaker, &c.
School House—Bright William, caretaker
Adult Schoolroom
22 Calder John, *Crown Inn*
24, 26 & 28 Watts Charles Ernest, hardware dealer
HERE IS COURT NO. 11
30 Dutfield James, shoemaker
32 Grazier Harry, general dealer
34 Sigley John, Son & Co., wholesale and manufacturing confectioners
36 Holt Thomas, butcher
38 Baylis George, hairdresser
40 Girls' Club
42 Tudor Coffee House, Ernest Wood, *Manager*
HERE IS COURT NO. 13
44 Lello Mrs. Mary, wardrobe dealer
46 Lello Mrs. Mary, baker
48 Burston Mrs. Harriet, furniture dealer
50 *Void*
52 Wright Thomas, hairdresser
54 Sandford Mrs. Mary Ann, wardrobe dlr.
56 Baddeley Ernest, tobaccnst. & newsagt.
58 Miller John, general dealer
60 & 62 Starkey John,boot and shoe repairer
64 McCowen John Thos., leather merchant and factor
HERE IS LICH STREET; ALSO SIDBURY

NEW STREET.
RIGHT SIDE FROM CHARLES STREET
1 Barnett John, Limited, corn and meal factors (Telephone No. 50A)—(see advt.)
2 Radford Frank Timon, eating house kpr.
3 Mapp George William, ironmonger
4 & 5 Baylis, Lewis & Co., printers
6 Yarnold Miss E., tripe dresser
7 Frost Mrs. Rebecca, wardrobe dealer
8 Frost Albert, antique dealer
9 *Warehouse void*
Liberal Club—Wm.Thos. Harris, *Manager*; Ernest Burgess, *Secretary*
10 *Void*
HERE IS NASH'S PASSAGE
11 Avery W. & T., Ltd., scale makers (branch repairing depôt)
12 Garbutt Frederick, jeweller
13 Jones Samuel W. H., electrician, &c.
14 Clackson Arthur, dealer in antiques
15 Fildes Thomas, cabinet maker and upholsterer
16 Atkinson Harvey, clothier, &c.
17 Seelhoff Oscar, confectioner
18 Bryant Charles Forbes, saddler
18A Smith & Co.'s Brush Warehouse
19 Bryant E. E., stationer
20 Hunting Henry William, coal and oil merchant
21 Brazier William H., baker, &c.
HERE IS WINDSOR ROW
22 Whiteley John, engraver
22 & 23 Hill Samuel & Son, trunk and umbrella manufacturers
{Cairns Martin, carpenter (workshop)
{Tomlins Chas.,general smith (workshop)
{Vaughan William, labourer
{Brittain Sydney, ironworker
24 Dinley John, agent for Sutton & Co., parcel carriers
25 Bird Alfred Edward, *Pheasant Inn*
Nichols Edwin & Co., Ltd., warehouse and workshop
26 Harris Sidney Thomas, printer
27 Nichols Edwin & Co., Ltd., antique furniture dealers, cabinet makers, &c. (See advt.)
28 Watkins Ernest, *Swan with Two Necks*
29 *Ye olde King Charles' House.* Wyatt Thos., dealer in antiques (see advt.)
30 Holtham & Co., corn & seed merchants
30 Hartwright Wm. Ed. (Holtham & Co.)
HERE IS THE OLD CORN MARKET
RETURN
Richardsons' Stores, Ltd. (office)
31 & 32 Goodwin T. K. & Son, Limited, wholesale grocers
33 Brittain Miss F. M., sweet shop
34 Gibbs Miss C. J., dressmaker
35 Parsons R. P., watchmaker & jeweller
36 Newell William, antique dealer
37 Yeast, Ltd., baker's utensils manufact'r
38 Millington E., ironmonger
39 Radford Thomas, fancy draper
40 & 41 Lewis Frederick, cycle dealer, &c.
42 Overton Fredk. L.,watch and clock mkr.
43 Haynes William Henry, hairdresser
44 *Void*
45 Rammell Mrs. A. H., wardrobe dealer
46 Silverthorn Henry, *Old Greyhound Inn*
47 Stinton Henry, basket manufacturer
48 Tredwell E. J., *New Greyhound Inn*
49 Laight Fredk. Geo., fancy dealer
50 Cam John, tobacconist
51 & 52 Wall Alfd. Geo.,wine & spirit vaults
HERE IS MARKET PASSAGE LEADING TO THE SHAMBLES
HERE IS THE BUTCHERS' MARKET
Meat and Hawkers' Market
City and County Arcade—Maggs Robert W., furniture dealer
Weights and Measures Office (open from 9 till 12)—W. R. Matthews, *Inspector*
53 Wall Bros., boot and shoe manufacturers
54 Elt's, ladies' outfitter
55 Thompson Mrs. Mary, fried fish shop
Nelson James & Sons, Ltd., butchers
HERE IS PUMP STREET; ALSO FRIAR STREET AND CHARLES STREET

Extracts from Littlebury's Street Directory, 1912 (left) and Kelly's Directory of 1928 (centre and right).

The Shambles, view along the east side, February 1966. Many of the traditional butchers' shops are there, including (right to left), Chas Smith & Son, James Andrews, George Mason, and Hales. (GNH)

Mealcheapen Street, St. Martin's Church and the Cornmarket area, view to the east from St. Swithin's Church tower, 15th April 1978. (CMH).

The north east corner of Trinity Street and Mealcheapen Street (right) c1920. In 1912, the businesses at this end of Mealcheapen Street included those of Miss E. M. Parsons, No 24 (at the point of closing down in this picture); James Nelson & Sons, butchers, No 23; Hunter's Tea Stores, No 22 and Rowland Smith, fruiterer, No 21. The name "Mealcheapen" derives from mealmarket. (CMHC).

The north east corner of Trinity Street and Mealcheapen Street, with Boots the Chemists, April, 1978.   (CMH).

The same aspect, 18th July 1996, with the controversial frontage of the Cheltenham & Gloucester building.   (CRH).

ABOVE
Mealcheapen Street in the 1970's, view to the west
with St. Swithin's Church at the far end and on the
right, the frontage of the one time Shades Inn. Built
in the mid 1700's, this imposing building has been a
private house, the first Post Office in the City, a
bank, restaurant and coffee house, it is now retail
premises. (CRH).

LEFT
The same view, 18th July 1996. (CRH).

Mealcheapen Street in the 1970's, view to the east, with many premises in a state of transition as development swept the street. To the right is the Radio, TV and hi-fi shop of John Life Ltd; next to that, Marsh & Baxters, butchers. (CRH)

From the same viewpoint,18th July 1996, pleasant and pedestrianised. (CRH).

The courtyard of The Reindeer Inn, Mealcheapen Street, c1980. The Reindeer was one of the City's coaching inns with carriers leaving throughout the day for destinations across the county. A pleasant City centre "watering place", it became absorbed into the Reindeer Court complex in the late 1980s. (CRH).

From the same viewpoint, 18th July 1996. The Mealcheapen Street access to Reindeer Court, an attractive and well mannered retail development leading to The Shambles and New Street. (CRH).

The Cornmarket, c1900. King Charles House stands at the north east (left hand) corner of New Street. This is the house from which King Charles II made his dramatic exit from the City, hotly pursued by Parliamentarian troops after the Battle of Worcester, 3rd September, 1651. The corner section, in brick, is the result of re-development of the whole site around 1800 but never completed. Public hangings and whippings once took place in The Cornmarket area. (CMHC).

The Cornmarket, view to the south east from the tower of St. Martin's Church, March 1967. W&F Webb's furniture store occupies the fine Georgian building which now houses the Worcester Furniture Exhibition Centre. (GNH).

The Cornmarket, view to the west, c1895. The Royal Exchange Inn is clearly visible at the corner of Mealcheapen Street. The Worcester Yeomanry are passing through, probably on a training patrol from their base in Silver Street. Pill-box style hats were issued to "other ranks" in 1892 and this helps to date the picture. The style was phased out around 1900. With the threat of Napoleonic invasion, Yeomanry units were formed across the country in 1794. The first volunteer unit in Worcester dates from this time. The Yeomanry assisted the civil authorities and militia in quelling riots and disturbances. (WEN).

The Plough Inn at the junction of The Cornmarket and St. Martin's Gate, c1935. The Plough was demolished to make way for the City Walls Road. Once called the White Horse Inn, it was one of twelve inns around The Cornmarket area. (BWJ).

ABOVE
The Public Hall, in the Cornmarket, was built in 1847 as a cornmarket but due to rivalry with The Corn Exchange, never fulfilled its function (see introduction to this chapter). It stands upon the site of the Wheatsheaf Inn where, under its colonnaded frontage, corn dealing would have taken place in the 18th century. At one time the City Pound for stray animals was just behind the building. A notice of 1603 reads "everye owner. . . .shall paye for everye such swyne and pygges soe taken the forfiture of 3s 4d". Here in 1966, the hall stands ready for demolition – to become a car park. (GNH).

ABOVE
The interior of the Public Hall, 1966 with organ (north end). (CMHC).

LEFT
The interior of the Public Hall, 1966 (south end). (CMHC).

LEFT
New Street, the east side, and a circus parade with an elaborate lion figure atop an ornate float. c1890. (AJB).

BELOW
Circus parade in The Cornmarket, c1890. A macabre spectacle, as a team of elephants pulls a cage containing the skeleton of another of their kind. (T)

Pawn tickets from 1934/5. J. Henry & Co had a branch at 9, The Cornmarket, with the main shop at 36, Broad Street. (CMHC).

New Street, 1912. The penny-farthing cycle is above Frederick Lewis's cycle shop. The timber framed building opposite is The Old Pheasant Inn, once the scene of many cockfights. (CMHC).

New Street, view to the north, 19th July 1996, complete with local colour – a juggler from Kaos, the juggling and circus acts shop in the street. (CRH).

ABOVE
The junction of Friar Street and Charles Street – a queue for groceries during the First World War. The building to the left of Thompsons, in Charles Street was the Cam Engineering Works. This part of Charles Street was created about 1895. The cross roads (with New St. to the north and Pump St. to the west) was once known as Ballam's Vine (sometimes called Baynhams Vine). (MS).

LEFT
Friar Street and the Greyfriars, view to the north, c1905. Part of the Greyfriars was an antique shop – " Ye Olde Curiositie Shoppe". (GNH).

Friar Street and the Greyfriars, view to the north, c1910. A picture full of life and bustle in this fine street. Just along on the left one can see the striped pole of a barbers shop (probably that of Henry Inchard) and the "lather boy", wearing an apron. (CMHC).

From the same viewpoint, 18th July 1996. (CRH).

LEFT
No. 27 Friar Street built around 1500, was near a gap in the City wall known as "Socket's Hole". It was bought by the Quakers in 1671, and a meeting house was built in the grounds. For about 100 years from around the mid 1700's, the house was used as a Quaker school. No. 27 is now, after considerable restoration, the bridal design shop "Perfections". Wyatt's Alms Houses (for "six aged honest poor men") were built behind this house in 1723. (JJC).

BELOW
Numbers 40 and 42 Friar Street (Tudor House), c1900. A substantial four bay building, it was built around 1600 as three clothiers' houses. For the technically-minded, the roof structure is clasped purlin, with three queen posts and straight wind braces. We can also see vertical marks in the wood beneath each first floor window indicating supports for bay windows. The building is presently The Museum of Local Life. (WC).

MR. WILLIAM LASLETT, M.P. FOR WORCESTER.—FROM A
PHOTOGRAPH BY J. WATKINS.

ABOVE: The central courtyard of the City Gaol, c1900, after conversion to almshouses by William Laslett in 1867-69. (HWCRO).

LEFT: William Laslett, a solicitor of Foregate Street, and a wealthy if somewhat eccentric benefactor of the City. He was Liberal MP in 1852, but failed to be re-elected in 1874. He could often be seen about the City wearing ragged clothes and could easily have been mistaken for a tramp. Wealthy though he was, he appeared to spend little on himself and would save on costs wherever possible. His gifts to the City included the 20 acres of land to provide Astwood Cemetery. (CMHC).

BELOW: Plan of Worcester City Gaol when in use as almshouses, May 1911. The chapel is clearly shown, as is the site of the treadmill. (HWCRO).

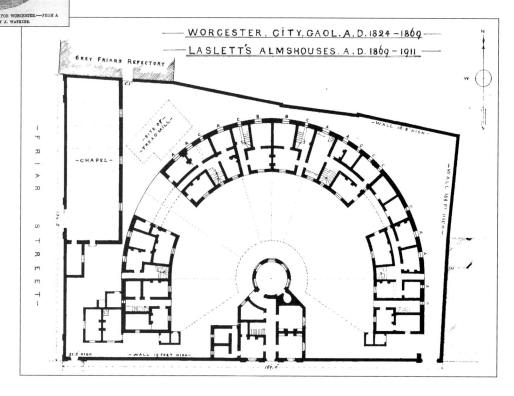

The corner of Friar Street and Union Street, view from the south c1900, with the old City Gaol entrance and the one-time gaol chapel behind the Friar Street wall. (CMHC).

From the same viewpoint, 18th July 1996. (CRH)

Laslett's Alms Houses c1912, shortly after their opening (HWCRO).

Pump Street (formerly Needler Street - another gloving industry association), c1940. To the right, beyond Russell & Dorrell's department store is the Wesleyan Church, built in the mid 1870s. It was the fourth Wesleyan church on the site and was demolished in 1966. The present church was opened in 1968. John Wesley regularly preached in the city during the late 1700's. (CMHC).

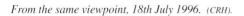

From the same viewpoint, 18th July 1996. (CRH).

Sidbury, view to the south c1900. The premises on the left have been demolished as far as Danesbury House (now Bygones Antiques Shop). The site has a literary association with the Victorian novelist, Mrs. Henry Wood (author of "East Lynne"). Hobson's sign protrudes a few doors down. Alfred Hobson was a hosier and outfitter. To the right stands the imposing frontage of The Angel Hotel with the Victoria Temperance Hotel next door to the right; the latter is now the Pescatore Restaurant which incorporates the ornate entrance from the demolished Angel Hotel. (CMHC).

From a similar viewpoint, 19th July 1996, showing the ornate canopy doorway of the one time Angel Hotel. (CRH)

ABOVE College Street, 1963. The east side, just prior to demolition. (GNH).

BELOW A cruck frame cottage (now demolished) at the corner of Kings Street (left) and Severn Street (right) c1870. (CMHC)

The junction of Sidbury and Edgar Street (on the left) c1905. The area was once known as The Knoll or Knolls End. Note the electric tram lines (installed along principal City routes 1903/04). At the corner with Edgar Street, the shop is that of G. Tetstal, Boot Repairer advertising gentlemen's boots soled and heeled for 2/6d (12 new pence). Next door to the right, is the tobacconist and newsagents shop of E. J. Lettice. The next but one building (white board at roofline) is in College Street and is the White Hart Inn (currently Shamus O'Donnell's) whilst the tall building, now with the upper storey modified, is that of J. F. Willis Ltd., shoe manufacturers, prior to their move to Watery Lane, St. Johns. (CMHC)

From the same viewpoint,19th July 1996. (CRH).

St. Peter's Street, Sidbury, looking west c1910. Every building in this picture has been demolished. St. Peter's Church was the last to go during the 1970's. (CMHC).

Sidbury, view to the north from near Wylds Lane, c1955. (HWCRO).

REFERENCES AND SOURCES

Barker, P., *A Short History of Worcester Cathedral* (1994)

Carver, M.O.H. (Ed.), *"Medieval Worcester" Transactions of The Worcestershire Archaeological Society,* 3rd series, vol. 7 (1980)

Craze, M., *The Old Palace, Worcester* (1984)

Green, V.A., *The History and Antiques of the City and Suburbs of Worcester* (1793)

Grundy, M., *Worcester Evening News*, "Memory Lane" series (1987-93)

Gwilliam, H.W., *Old Worcester: People and Places* (1993)

Haynes, C.R. & M.L.D. with Adlam, B., *Yesterday's Town: The Changing Face of Worcester* (1978)

Haynes, C.R. & M.L.D., *Old Worcester as seen through the Camera* (1986)

Hughes, P. (Ed)., *Blackfriars* (1986)

Hughes, P., *Worcester Walkabout – Cornmarket, New Street and Friar Street* (1985)

Hughes, P. & Molyneux, N.,*Worcester Streets: Friar Street* (1984)

Moore Ede, Dr. W., *Worcester Cathedral* (1934) with revisions by Dr. F. E. Hutchinson

Morriss, R.K. & Hoverd, K., *The Buildings of Worcester* (1994)

Nash, T., *Collections for the History of Worcestershire* (1781)

Roslington, C. (Ed.), *The Kings School, Worcester and a History of its Site* (1994)

Spackman, F.T., *The Ancient Monuments and Historic Buildings of Worcester* (1913)

Whitehead, D., *The Book of Worcester* (1976)

Kelly's Directory of Worcester (1928)

Littlebury's Directory of Worcester (1912)

INDEX

Abbey National plc, 44
Abell & Smith Electrical Co. Ltd., 15,40
Albion House, 37
Albion, The, 86
All Hallows, 11,13,70
All Saints Church, 10,47,52,105
All Saints Road, 11,25,45
All Saints Workhouse, 88
Allies, James, 12
Almshouses, 146
Angel Hotel, 149
Angel Lane, 17
Angel Mall, 26
Angel Passage, 106
Angel Place, 11,14,15,17,21-24,26,29,32,41
Angel Row, 17
Angel Street, 21,33,35,106,127
Atalanta, 68

Badger, J. & W., ironmonger, 126
Ballam's Vine, 143
Bank Street, 50,51,70,116
Barnett's clothing shop, 127
Barrels Wine Bar, 20
Bathing Barge, 89
Beard's food emporium, 44
Beatties department store, 52
Beauchamp Hotel, 36
Beesley, Edward, 50
Bell Hotel, 22,40
Benedictine Order, 92
Berkeley Arms Inn, 116
Berrow's Worcester Journal, 41
Birdport, 11,13,48,50,70
Birley & Co, jeweller, 108,111
Bishop's Palace, 102
Blackfriars,11,12,16,18,21,24,25,36,28,70,114
     shopping centre, 29,31
     multi-storey car park, 20,33
     market hall, 30
     Safeway Supermarket, 30

Boots the Chemists, 133
Bosel, 91,103
Bradburn's Doll's Hospital, 118
Bread Dole, 97
Bridge
     Sabrina footbridge, 57,86,89
     railway bridge, 57,85,86
     road bridge, 60-65,80
Bridge Street, 57,70,82,105
Broad Street, 22,24,28,36,37,40-45,70,115
Broadcloth, 12
Bull Entry, 11,48,51
Butchers Arms, 129
Butchers Market, 128
Butts Siding, 59
Butts Spur line, 57,84
Butts, The, 14,18,19,25

Canal, 56
Capital & Counties Bank, 111
Cassidy's, jeweller, 108,110,111
Castle Hill, 66,101
Cathedral, 66,90-99
     Cloisters, 92
     Lady Chapel, 92,99
     Nave, 98
     Quire, 92,99
Cathedral Choir, 96
Cathedral Ferry, 77
Cathedral Library, 93
Cattle Market, 10,18
Chapel Walk, 11,51
Chapter House, 92
Charles Street, 143
Cheltenham & Gloucester plc, 133
Church Army, 97
Church Street, 105,128
Circus parade, 140
City Ambulance Station, 50,52
City Coat of Arms, 64
City Gaol, 106,146,147

City Police Station, 48
City Pound, 139
City Rag Stores, 50
City Wall, 14,19
Civet Cat, public house, 108
Clothiers Trade Guild, 12
Cold Bath, 19
College Hall, 92
College of Technology, 48,70,71,74
    Powick Lane annexe, 50
College Street, 123,125,150
Congregational Church, 17
Copenhagen Street, 12,13,48,66,67,70,78,79,81
Corn Exchange, 105-106
Cornmarket, The, 105-106,132,137-140
Countess of Huntingdon's Church, 12,48,53
Cripplegate Park, 64
Cross, The, 44,105,107,108,109,115
Crown Hotel, 43
Crowngate, 12,28,37,42,48,50,51,81
    multi-storey carpark, 20

Deansway, 11,13,37,48,52,54,55,70,81
Deansway Restaurant, 54
Dent's Glove Factory, 60,67,69,71
Diglis, 75
Dingle, Son & Edwards, wine merchants, 40
Dolday, 10,11,25,87,88
Dominican Friary, 10,11,14
Duke of Wellington Inn, 48,53

Eden, A.F., fruiterer & fishmonger, 37
Edgar Street, 151
Edgar Tower, 92,102,103
Edwards, Charles, wine merchants, 23
Elgar Music and Pianoforte shop, 120
Elgar School of Music, 12,53
England's Shoes, 127
Ewe and Lamb Inn, 18
Eyeport, 11

Farriers Arms, 55
Ferries, 77
Firkins & Co, hop merchants, 68
Fish Street, 55
Five Ways, 17,21
Flight & Barr, porcelain works, 71
Foregate, The, 126,127
Foss's Corn & Seed Merchant, 128
Franciscan Friars, 106

Friar Street, 106,122,143-145,147
Friars Orchard, 17
Friars Alley, 11,12
Friary Walk, 31
Fruit and Vegetable Market, 21,26

George & Welch, pharmacists, 44
Giffard Hotel, 123
Glenn's, gents outfitters, 43
Golden Cross, 107
Grammar School for Girls, 19
Great Western Railway, 86
Green Dragon, 46
Greig, David, grocer, 114
Greyfriars, The, 106,143,144
Grimaldi, 34
Group Lane, 54,70
Guesten Hall, 92,100
Guildhall, 48,105,117
Gwynne, John, 57,63

Halfords, 41
Hall, J. & F., ironmonger, 128
Hall's, silversmith, 122
Handley, Henry, 123
Hardman, 92
Hares Lane, 70
Herefordshire House Inn, 45,46
Heroes Restaurant, 106
High Street, 105,110-114,118,120-121,124-125
Hill's Famous Boots shop, 110
Hobson, Alfred, 149
Hollybush Inn, 126
Homoeopathic Dispensary, 17
Hood Street, 74
Hope and Anchor, 46
Hopkins, W.H., & Co., bakers, 37
Hounds Lane School, 70,78
Hunt's, fishmongers, 110
Hylton Road, 80,85

Industrial Revolution, 56
International Stores, 41

J. Henry & Co, pawnbroker, 141
J.F. Willis Ltd, shoe manufacturers, 151
James Cafe, The, 45
Jap Co. , 41
Jeynes, William, general stores, 67
Jones, A.O., stationers, 41

Keen, Edmund, 34
Kembles, The, 34
King Charles House, 137
King John, 92
Kings Street, 150
Knoll, The, 151
Kwik Save Supermarket, 33,34

Laslett's Alms Houses, 106,147
Laslett, William, 106,146
Lea & Perrins, 44
Leland, John, 12
Leonard, E., family grocer, 38
Lewis Clarke's Brewery, 12,14-17,20
Lewis, F., cycle shop, 142
Lich Gate, 119
Lich Street, 119,122,124
Little Angel Street, 11,17,21,22,40
Little Fish Street, 70
Loynes, building supplies, 51
Lucking, James & Co., opticians, 43

Majestic, The, 106
Marks & Spencer, 110
Maypole Dairy Co, 109
McCowan's leather goods shop, 122
Mealcheapen Street, 132-138
Mellor's Sauce Factory, 60
Merryvale, 11,13,50,70
Modern Fireplaces, 37
Moore, J, marine stores, 68
Morton Square, 11,16
Morton, Richard, 12
Mothercare, 44
Motor Taxation Office, 48
Museum of Local Life, 145

Netherton Lane, 25
New Road, 57,62,89
New Street, 106,137,140,142
Newport Street, 10,11,25,45,46,47,57,61,88
North Parade, 57,60,83
North Quay, 46,57,59,60
North Wall House, 19,20
Norton & Whitton, confectioners, 51
Norwich Union, 17

Old Pheasant Inn, The, 142
Old Rectifying House, 60,64
Old Red Lion, 46

Old St Michael's Church, 94
Oxford, Worcester & Wolv'mpton Railway, 86

Palace Yard, 11,13
Palmer, G.A., & Sons, fruiterer & florist, 37
Pawn tickets, 141
Paynes Meadow, 77
Pearl Assurance, 43
Pemberton's Brush Factory, 12,18,24
Pembroke's Brush Factory, 10
Phipson, Evacustes, 46
Phoenix Fire Engine House, 17
Pitchcroft, 19
Plough Inn, 138
Police Station, 12
Pollard, Herbert E., & Co., gun makers, 43
Porcelain factory, 66
Power Station, 25,80
Powick Lane, 12,49,50-52,70
Prince Arthur's Chantry, 92
Prosser, William, rag merchant, 50
Public Hall, 106,139
Pump Street, 148

Quakers, 145
Quay Street, 55,74
Quayside, 57

Rack Alley, 11,12
Reindeer Court, 136
Reindeer Inn, 136
River Severn, 19,56,76
Round houses, 57
Royal Exchange Inn, 138
Royal Infirmary, 58
Rush Alley, 57

Samuel, H., jeweller, 109
Scala Cinema, 26,27
Scott, Sir George Gilbert, 92
Severn Street, 150
Severn View Hotel, 46
Shades Inn, 134
Shadrath Pride, 19
Shakespeare Hotel, 33
Shambles, The, 128,129,131
Sheep Market, 17,26
Shuter & Flays, grocers, 114
Sidbury, 122,149,151-153
Siddons, Sarah, 34

Sigley's Sweet Factory, 106
Simes Department Store, 111,114
Skan & Sons, tobacconists & barbers, 43,44
Skating, 76
Smock Alley, 11,12,14,16
South Parade, 66,73,74,84
South Quay, 57,67,68,71,72
Sow and Pig Inn, 88
St Alban's Church, 91
St Alban's Square, 81
St Andrew's, 70,71,81
St Andrew's Institute, 67
St Clement's Church, 58,88
St Helen's Church, 91
St Lawrence' Church, 106
St Margaret's Church, 91
St Martin's Church, 105,132
St Martin's Gate, 138
St Michael's Church, 123
St Nicholas' Church, 105,107,126
St Oswald, 91,103
St Peter's Church, 152
St Swithin's Church, 105,108,129
St Wulfstan, 91,103
Stallard's Worcester Distillery, 69
Steps Cafe Bar, 53
Stewart's Shop, 109
Street Directories, 106,130

Take "A" Break Cafe, 45
Theatre Royal, 33-35
Thomas Edwin Blackford's drapery, 43
Tilley, Vesta, 34,35
Toll house, 57,62,65
Toll tickets, 65
Trams
    electric, 36,82,109,115,151
    horse, 89,107
Trinity Street, 132,133
Tudor House, 106,145
Turkey, 57,61
Tybridge Street, 11,57,61

Unicorn Chambers, 42
Unicorn Hotel, 42
Union Street, 106,147
Upper Butts Brewery, 12

Vaults Hotel, 21
Vaults Inn, 15
Victoria Temperance Hotel, 149

W. H. Smith, 127
W. & F. Webb & Co, furnishers, 113
Wark, James, 12
Warmstry Court, 73,74
Warmstry Slip, 69,70
Water Gate, 77,92
Waterman's Chapel, 10,86,87
Webb's Horse Hair Carpet Factory, 13,48
Webb, Edward, 13,48
Well, The, 11,13
Wellington Square, 88
Wesleyan Church, 148
West Midlands Railway, 86
Wherry Inn, 67,68
White Hart Inn, 151
Whitts, general draper, 113
Wintle's timber yard, 83
Wooden Stair Street, 74
Woolpack Inn, 88
Woolworth & Co., 110
Worcester Bank, 107
Worcester Toy Shop, 118
Worcester Young Farmers, 117
Worcestershire Sauce, 44
Wyatt's Alms Houses, 145

Ye Olde Curiositie Shoppe, 143
Ye Olde Punch Bowl Inn, 119
Young Roscium, 34